Libraries, Information and Archives

This item is to be returned on or before the last date shown below

WS

Being

Cadila

We Are Unstoppable

Being

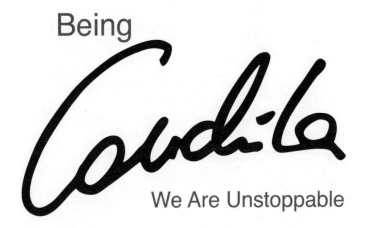

We Are Unstoppable

As told to Daniel Oliver Bachmann

JOHN BLAKE

Published by John Blake Publishing Ltd,
3 Bramber Court, 2 Bramber Road,
London W14 9PB, England

www.johnblakepublishing.co.uk

www.facebook.com/johnblakebooks 🖪
twitter.com/jblakebooks 🄴

Originally published in Germany as *Ich, Conchita, Meine Geschichte aufgeschrieben und erzuhlt von Daniel Oliver Bachmann* © LangenMuller, Munchen, 2015

This edition published in hardback in 2015

ISBN: 978 1 78418 649 4

British Library Cataloguing-in-Publication Data:

A catalogue record for this book is available from the British Library.

Design by www.envydesign.co.uk

Printed in Great Britain by CPI Group (UK) Ltd

1 3 5 7 9 10 8 6 4 2

Picture cr...   ...ig Photography
     Back...   ...ko Badzic
Page 1, 2, ...Family Archive

     Page ...   ...urst, 2014
Page 25 ...   ...zy Horse Paris
                                                                ...e

The righ...   ...work has been
     asserte...   ...Designs and

Papers us...   ...icts made from
wood gr...   ...onform to the

Every attempt has been made to contact the relevant copyright-holders, but some were unobtainable. We would be grateful if the appropriate people could contact us.

CONTENTS

LETTER FROM
JEAN-PAUL GAULTIER

Paris, 12 December 2014

Dear Conchita,

The first time I saw you was on the internet when you were in the selection process to be the Austrian representative of the Eurovision Song Contest. It was like a jolt, like a shock to me and also a revelation. The look, the voice… I was seduced and wanted to get to know you immediately. I invited you to come to Paris and see my show and when I met you and talked to you I became your unconditional fan. It was a *coup de foudre*. And I also discovered that your name had a double, even triple meaning.

Two years later you sang for Austria and the rest is history. I voted for you seventy-three times! Your victory was not only for a song, a singer, an incredible voice and a fantastic interpretation, but also a victory for the values in which I believe in and for which I fought throughout my career:

tolerance and humanity. This was a victory for all those who are different, as well as a message of encouragement to them to express their difference, to manifest it and to live it. You are a unique human being, positive and generous, smart and straightforward.

Like Madonna who is a real macho in a woman's body, you are a Wonder Woman in a man's body. You erase boundaries between masculine and feminine like no one did before. You succeeded, coming from the avant-garde and the underground, to become a popular icon, and a fashion icon forever. I look up to you for how you break the fashion codes like I did throughout my career: the male and female duality, male object and strong woman.

Conchita, you are a true inspiration and I am proud to know you and to be your friend.

Jean Paul Gaultier

PROLOGUE

The night before the grand final of the Eurovision Song Contest, I stood in front of the mirror in my hotel room. For the first time in many hours I was completely alone – well, almost. Getting ready for a short night's sleep, my face half free of makeup, I gazed into the glass at the shape-shifter I knew so well. At someone who inspires joy, tolerance and love in so many, and yet who also stirs up hatred, anger and fear of the most important question there is: who am I? It was a question I asked myself that night. Who am I, and who will I be for the time it takes to sing a song, when I take to the stage tomorrow night with the eyes of the world fixed upon me? Who will I be for those three minutes? Those three minutes that could become an eternity in the unlikely event that I win. 'If that happens, then you and I have a problem,' I told the hybrid in the mirror. 'If that happens, we have to come up with something intelligent to say.'

Conchita gave me a smile. Or was it Tom Neuwirth, the country boy, the boy who grew up far from the glare of the spotlights? The boy from a place where people take their holidays, where all's still right with the world – or so they say. If that were really the case, though, then how do you explain Conchita?

I reached for another piece of cotton wool and carried on removing my makeup. Conchita retreated with every dab, making way for Tom. Going round in my head was the song I'd be performing the following day. It tells of the ancient legend of the phoenix, a mythical bird that bursts into flame at the end of its life only to rise again from the ashes. The phoenix is itself based on the ancient Egyptian bird god *Bennu*, a deity who represented eternal life and was hence also known as the 'reincarnated son'. It's him I see in the mirror as Conchita disappears along with her makeup: it's the rebirth of Tom, the boy from the sticks. By this point my wig has long been put aside; my dress hangs from the clothes rail. A few more dabs and Conchita will be gone.

'We have to come up with something intelligent,' I repeat.

Perhaps a spot of eye-shadow fell into my eye. Perhaps it was some of the mascara that Conchita so likes. Whatever it was, tears started streaming down my face, and suddenly Tom was a young boy again, a boy in shorts and rolled-down socks, with a T-shirt pulled over his skinny frame. The air was filled with the fresh scent of pine and the sound of water from a trickling stream. Little Tom jumped across the stream and ran on as fast as his legs could carry him, and running along beside him was happiness, a happiness known only to those who've experienced one of those country summers that seem, in the eyes of a child, to last forever.

'Why make it up?' I heard Conchita ask. 'Just tell them your story. There's no point trying to say something intelligent unless you've experienced it for yourself.' And so, as she's usually right, I wrote myself a note: If I win, I tell my story. But only *if*.

CHAPTER ONE

THE GREEN CAVE

'I want to make magic,
I want to electrify the place'
FROM THE MUSICAL *FAME*

My life is a musical, I often say. For one thing, it began where so many musicals begin: in the countryside. What's more, it features music and singing, drama and comedy – and then there's my love of cabaret, with all its costumes and mesmerising stories. One of my very first memories feels as though it was lifted straight from a musical: I was four years old, and we were living in Ebensee, a romantic little town on the southern bank of Traunsee lake, in the centre of the Salzkammergut region of Austria. In this memory of mine, I can see boats sailing across the water, while a cable car wends its way up to the plateau at Feuerkogel. Further up is Rindbach waterfall, which turns into a raging torrent in spring, and the stalagmite cave at Gassenkogel, its entrance a thousand metres above the lake.

Yet there was another cave, one that existed inside our house, an enchanted villa the size of a fairytale castle. In real life, our house was a youth hostel run by my parents, with a common room upholstered from floor to ceiling in soft, forest green. The whole room was like a moss-covered cave, and it was where the groups of school children that filled our house held their parties. When no one else was around, the cave belonged to me. It then became a space in which to play and to dream, somewhere that was home to giants and dwarves, fairies and elves. It was there that I sensed the existence of a life that went beyond the 'reality' of which the adults loved to speak. Whole worlds could be created in the blink of an eye, worlds that only a child could see. Years later, when I returned for a visit after we'd moved, the cave had disappeared. Somebody had torn the upholstery down from the walls and set to work with a paintbrush and paint. Now it was merely a room that was inoffensive enough, but totally devoid of creativity, of the possibility of travelling to other worlds. This sort of thing happens a lot: we renovate a place to death and are then surprised when our inspiration runs dry. There'd never been any chance of that happening to me in the Green Cave. No wonder it had been so hard to say goodbye. My father had set up his own restaurant and so we'd had to leave Ebensee. Back then, I had no way of knowing that another cave of fantasies lay waiting for me in my new home, one that was also resplendent with green, with the colour of hope and of immortality. It's the sort of thing that usually only happens in musicals – or in my life.

CHAPTER TWO

TROUBLE IN PARADISE

'Hiding away,
There's a little bit of gypsy in me'
FROM THE MUSICAL *ANYTHING GOES*

We moved from one paradise to another: our new hometown of Bad Mitterndorf was, just like Ebensee, situated in the heart of the Salzkammergut region, surrounded by mountains, meadows and forests. Once again, we weren't far from water, being close to the Salza reservoir and the thermal springs of Heilbrunn, where the Romans used to bathe. In winter, people would come from all over the world to go skiing on the Tauplitzalm. Those who were really brave would cross to the Kulm, the world's largest natural jumping hill, where jumps of over 200 metres are not out of the ordinary. I spent my childhood playing out in the fresh air with my brother Andi, who's one-and-a-half years my senior, and our friends. On returning home breathless, hungry and thirsty, we'd be allowed to pick a meal from the menu at

3

my parent's restaurant. At the time, I didn't understand why our playmates looked so envious – it was something we just took for granted. Looking back on this period, it seems like one long childhood dream. Quite recently, my mother told me how sorry she was that she and my father had had so little time for us as children. They'd been busy knocking the restaurant into shape and building up their business. I was able to put her mind at rest, because I'd had a completely different experience of things: whenever we'd needed our parents, they'd been there for us. That never changed, not even when my life in Bad Mitterndorf took a turn for the worse and trouble began to brew in paradise.

It all started at puberty. All of a sudden, my life contained an element of uncertainty that I had never known before. I can no longer say who was the first to notice that I was different to my classmates: me or them. Teenagers have a sixth sense for 'otherness', and, at a stage in life when everyone still wants to be the same as everyone else, the term 'different' is a form of insult. I started to hear more and more of these, since sooner or later most of the boys in my class came to the conclusion that there was something not quite right about Tom. Exactly what that was remained unclear, but there was a term for it nonetheless: *gay*.

It was a word flung around in every conceivable variation, even though none of the loudmouths who used it actually knew what it meant. This isn't so surprising when you consider that, even today, we don't know for sure when or why this word became synonymous with *homosexual*. I did look it up once: the German word for *gay* (*schwul*) is thought to be derived from Rotwelsch, a dialect that originated in the Middle Ages among travelling merchants, craftsmen, tinkers and pedlars. And *homosexual*? A word coined in 1869 by the Austro-Hungarian writer Karl Maria Kertbeny by combining the Greek word *homós* with the Latin word *sexus*. It translates roughly as *same-sex*, which explains some things, though by no means everything. But the boys at my school weren't bothered about all that: for them, the main thing was to point the finger at the gay. As I now know, this often reflects a great fear of being gay oneself.

The mess in which we humans find ourselves stems from having rules we don't understand. Homosexuality was banned in our culture from the time of the early Christians, leading to persecution, execution and, ultimately, to the madness of the Nazis, who thought that all gays belonged in concentration camps. For more than 120 years, Paragraph 175 was enshrined in German law, making homosexual acts between men a crime punishable by imprisonment. I didn't know any of this this back then. Deep inside, I felt that being gay was neither dirty nor wrong. When I stand up for tolerance and love today, what I say is essentially the same as what I already felt all that time ago: we humans come from many different nations and cultures, have many different skin colours and features – and we're always right.

My school years in Bad Mitterndorf taught me what happens when we banish this tolerance from our lives. More often than not, it was small acts of cruelty – whispering behind my back, or calling out insults as I walked past. While these experiences left their mark, they didn't embitter me. But it doesn't always work out that way: I'll never forget hearing the following story, one that illustrates clearly where being let down by others can lead. It concerns Muhammad Ali – possibly the greatest heavyweight boxer of all time, 'Sportsman of the Century', and recipient of the Presidential Medal of Freedom and the Otto Hahn Peace Medal for 'outstanding services to peace and international understanding'. After winning his gold medal in the 1960 Olympics in Rome, the eighteen-year-old returned home to Louisville with these words on his lips: 'I've won for my country.' But it was a country still rife with discrimination and racial segregation and, on entering a milk bar, Ali found himself thrown out to applause from the guests. He knew then what his achievement was worth in the eyes of the whites: nothing. In his frustration, he took his gold medal and hurled it into the Ohio River. He also refused to fight for America in Vietnam, a decision that led to decades of demonisation.

In 2014, I was offered honorary citizenship of Bad Mitterndorf. It was because I hadn't become embittered by my experiences that I was able to accept. I sensed that something had taken root in the hearts and minds of those who used to single me out: the realisation that it's OK to be different. None of us can tell what the future holds, and it's probably better that way. Maybe we would just give up if we saw the difficulties that life has in store for us. Every morning when getting ready for schol, whenever my thoughts turned to the day ahead, I felt like I was going to be sick. During class, I could hardly wait for the bell to go. I was constantly stressed, and felt defenceless against the mocking stares and torrents of abuse from my classmates. There was nothing I could do to fight back, as the balance of power was clearly in their favour. There were many of them and just one of me

– or at least that's the way it seemed. I later learned that the reality was somewhat different, after hearing enough stories about seemingly normal fathers who'd left their families to finally be true to their nature. Back in my school days, however, it felt like everybody else looked down upon and hated gays. Still, I had an easier time of it than some. I was never beaten up, though this can happen to you for a variety of reasons when you're young. Florian, my best friend at the time, hit the nail on the head: 'You don't need to be gay to have a hard time at school,' he commented. 'Having glasses and braces is enough.'

Nonetheless, I still felt excluded when break time came around and all the other boys ran off to the toilets to lie in wait for me there. 'What's gay boy's one like, eh?' 'Is it different?' 'Let's show him a bit of a hard time, boys.' In the end, I only went to the toilets during class, something which didn't make me too popular with the teachers – who, I should add, didn't do much to protect me from my tormentors.

There was never a lack of opportunity to stare at and make fun of me. Even the yearly fire drill. As soon as the siren on the school roof started to sound, we had to file out of the building class by class and then line up in orderly rows outside. There was always a lot of pushing and shoving going on around where I was standing, around the boy who was different, the boy who was gay. Little by little, I managed to create safety zones, building a cordon of girls around me. My relationship with the girls boiled down to this: I loved them and they loved me. Lots of the boys at school envied how relaxed I was in my interactions with members of the opposite sex. 'Why *him* of all people?' they would ask themselves, although the answer was obvious: I took the girls seriously, and they did me. I started developing an increasingly close friendship with one girl in particular, Kristin, which has lasted to this day. Kristin and I did duets together, and we were an unbeatable duo. We performed at school fairs, speech days, festivals – you name it – and I became sought after as an organiser, director and performer at these events. I'd jump at the chance to go on stage or to sing, particularly as it gave me the opportunity to pursue a growing passion of mine. I loved materials and dresses, and had a talent for making novel creations with a needle and thread. Add Kristin into the equation and our performances soon became a hit. We usually went onstage wearing the same outfit, and had to hide our laughter whenever someone remarked: 'You two are twins, right?'

That we weren't even sisters can be seen in an old photo taken at our first holy communion. As we stand before our families and the rest of the congregation to receive the gift of Christ's body and blood – a miracle the adults couldn't explain away – the photo shows us trussed up in the clothes that are standard for this event. The boys are wearing suits that make them look like miniature men, while the girls are in dresses that look like bridal gowns. I sit forlorn, one hand around my candle and the other on Kristin's dress, my gaze resting on its delicate lacework. Looking at the photo today, I suspect I was envious. I was probably thinking that I ought to be wearing such a pretty dress too. I put on my mum's and my grandma's wedding dresses at home to make up for it, and cut up a dress belonging my aunt so I could turn it into something better.

I can't remember exactly when it was that I started slipping into women's clothes. I was able to do so only because my parents accepted it completely, showing me an unconditional love that I try to take with me into the world today. It also helped that I had a fresh opportunity for my fantasies to take shape: once again there was a Green Cave and once again it was a space where I could let my creativity run free. This time, the cave was up in the loft, and with the help of some old mattresses, unwanted carpets and discarded pieces of furniture (including one ancient mirror I still remember), Andi and I slowly converted it into a child's paradise. Whenever our cousins came to visit, the adults always knew where we'd be hiding out. 'The kids are upstairs,' became a standard phrase in our household. We would spend hours on end flying from one fantasy world into the next. Later on, when Andi went away to boarding school in Bad Ischl, the cave underwent a transformation. It now became my creative studio, where I could indulge my passion for singing to my heart's content, while coming up with designs for wonderful dresses. Theory has always been less important to me than practice, and I soon began creating clothes from my designs. I remember Andi coming home one day with the news that Bad Ischl was where the Austrian Emperor Franz Joseph had become engaged to the Bavarian Duchess Elisabeth Amalie Eugenie, better known as 'Sisi'. On hearing this, I immediately threw on a dress that would have been suitable for the occasion.

I had some wonderful times up in my cave, but I wasn't blind to the fact that it was really my hiding place: I was keeping myself hidden from the eyes of Bad Mitterndorf. Even back then, I knew this was no way to live my life. That's why, after finishing school at the age of fourteen, I decided to leave. Even though I was already a keen singer, the idea of going to somewhere like Vienna and studying at a conservatoire or music academy never crossed my mind. Nowadays, of course, they have proper processes for picking out children who are musically talented, making it easier for them to enter those kinds of establishment. They ask questions about whether the child has a strong affinity with music and sounds, whether they prefer expressing themselves through the medium of music, and whether they have a tendency to spend their time in musical activities. All of these things applied to me, but, at the time, the world of music was still too far removed from my own.

With fashion it was a different story: both my parents and I saw dressmaking as a good, solid trade. One possibility was the Graz School of Fashion, which described itself as preparing students for 'a career in industry, especially in the fashion industry'. Compared to Bad Mitterndorf, which had a population of 3,000, Graz would seem like a great metropolis. It was the state capital of Styria, which had become the fastest growing conurbation in Austria. These were factors that gave my parents cause for hesitation. Yet when it came down to it, they remembered having to stand on their own two feet when they were younger, so they knew that not all professions can be learnt in one's hometown. Once they were assured that I'd be staying somewhere 'decent', Mum and Dad supported me to take my step into the unknown, and for this I respect them.

CHAPTER THREE

WITH NEEDLE AND THREAD

'No need to come back at all'

FROM THE MUSICAL AT *HOME ABROAD*

'Now I can be my true self.'

These were the words going through my head as I arrived in Graz, knowing next to nothing about the town. Without a doubt, it was a metropolis compared to the country idyll I'd left behind,. However, this image of it was soon put into perspective. It was true that Graz had everything that Bad Mitterndorf lacked – there were clubs, discos, bars and lounges – but these held little attraction to a fourteen-year-old boy from the country. My belief that this was somewhere that I could be my true self arose entirely from my desire to no longer be stared at, bullied and left out. I would have bet everything I owned that my new life would not be like that. It turned out that I was mistaken. The very opposite was true.

The 'somewhere decent' my parents had banked on was

a boarding house shared between students from the fashion school and other youngsters attending one of Graz's many secondary schools or doing apprenticeships. It was a four-storey building with boys on the lower floors and girls on the upper ones and an impassable divide between them, like the old barrier between East and West. The strict ban on visitors was there to give the head of the boarding house some peace of mind, but it was completely ineffectual. In any case, my feelings towards the female boarders were completely different to those held by the rest of the boys, with their rocketing testosterone levels. While they were struggling with acne, wet dreams and delusions about what they'd be doing to the girls if given half the chance, the residents of the upper floors became my best friends. And so the madness of my school days picked up where it had left off. Since the boy/girl dividing line was a strictly monitored operation, it meant that most of the boys needed some sort of emotional outlet. It turned out that this outlet was me. The boy that was different. The boy that was gay.

While I was never beaten up in Graz, psychological abuse can be more hurtful than any physical injury. From Monday to Friday, I was at the mercy of my housemates. On Friday afternoons, I would take a two-hour train to Stainach-Irdning, change to the local service for Bad Mitterndorf and arrive there half an hour later. If I was unlucky, I'd cross paths with someone whose main pleasure in life was harassing people like me before I'd even managed to leave the station. It's not really surprising that I spent most of my time up in the attic once more, in the Green Cave – much to the benefit of my vocal skills and my proficiency with a needle and thread. I was able to hone my abilities as a designer and dressmaker, sailing through fashion school as a result. As for my singing, it was in the attic that I built the foundations for translating talent into success.

I was recently reading American author Malcolm Gladwell's book *Outliers: The Story of Success*, in which he describes a study carried out by the psychologist Anders Ericsson. In *The Making of an Expert*, Ericsson establishes that so-called 'high-flyers' don't actually start life as geniuses: their success is down to hard work and discipline. We now know that it takes ten thousand hours of practice to become a top singer, pianist, violinist, writer or athlete. Ten thousand hours sounds a lot, and it is, but if you're passionate about something then it's achievable. It's this quality – this being passionate about something – that separates the wheat from the chaff. If you put in four hours of dedicated practice a day – which isn't much for an aspiring singer – you fulfil the quota in 2,500 days. With your average working day of eight hours, it takes 1,250 days, or three-and-a-half years. I don't consider myself a 'high-flyer', despite what many people were saying after my Eurovision victory. To some people, those who hadn't heard of me until that point, I was like a phoenix rising out of the ashes and into the spotlight. Staying with this imagery a moment longer, it's worth remembering that the phoenix has already had a previous life. In my case, it was definitely not the life of a high-flyer. It was a life of hard graft. When I came home for the weekend, the attic became my vocal studio, a place where I spent hour upon hour upon hour training my voice.

I often get asked the following question, whether in person

or via social media: 'Should I pursue my talent, Conchita?'
My answer is neither 'Go for it!' nor 'Definitely not!' I
point people in a different direction: if you want to clock
up your ten thousand hours of practice, you really need to
derive a sense of fun and enjoyment from what you're doing.
That's the secret of success. If you're enjoying yourself and
you bring that feeling into your singing, into practising an
instrument, into whatever it is you're doing, then sooner or
later you'll reap the rewards. What needs to accompany this
enjoyment is the discipline to persevere even when things
aren't going as well as they could be. It's a lesson I had to
learn for myself.

So it was that I spent Friday evenings, Saturdays and
Sundays in the Green Cave, up in the attic back home. It
wasn't the easiest of situations for my parents. Being able to
successfully run a country restaurant is dependent on local
interest; my mother and father couldn't simply be indifferent
to the residents of Bad Mitterndorf and their opinions – or,
as we say in Austria and southern Germany, they couldn't
just not give a toss (*es war ihnen keinesfalls wurst*). I had no
idea back then that these tensions would one day contribute
to my choice of stage name. My parents have my respect
for managing to navigate the sometimes irreconcilable
chasm between the demands of society and what they
themselves believed. While I was up in the attic practising
my arias, downstairs they were serving up plates of steaming
dumplings along with pint after pint of beer. It was a collision
of two different worlds. Thankfully, these worlds no longer
stand as far apart as they used to, but back then they were
separated by another one of those impassable divides. From

time to time, I would cross over to the other side and enter into restaurant life, mostly by doing a performance or putting on a small fashion show. Yet no-one ever crossed onto my side of the barrier. The only people who came up to visit me were relatives and close friends. The Green Cave was my shelter, and it remained so for a long time.

At carnival time the situation was different. Bad Mitterndorf was a town that always honoured its traditions, and one of these was the raising of the maypole. On the evening of 30 April, a 30- to 35-metre-high tree was cut down and then lifted into position with the assistance of most of the town. The tree had to be guarded overnight, a ritual stemming from the old custom of ripping down the maypoles of neighbouring villages. When the band came marching through town the following morning – with me blasting away joyfully on the clarinet – it marked the end of possible enemy capture. Throughout this period, business in the restaurant was booming, and it was the same at carnival time.

The 'fifth season', as it was universally known, became a time of joyful exuberance for me. I was suddenly allowed to do what I'd always wanted: to dress however I liked and celebrate alongside other people without having to keep monitoring myself. While the carnival tradition is associated with the idea of casting out the winter, it has its origins in a type of medieval court where commoners could vent their grievances against their masters. When you look at it in this light, carnival time could basically have been created with me in mind! Yet as soon as the celebrations were finished, I had to return to my hide-out in the attic. I would go back to my singing exercises, to my world of fabric, needle and thread, where I spent Sundays anxiously peering at the hands of the clock as they ticked mercilessly on towards three o'clock. That was when I had to take the train back to Graz, to boarding school, to the boundary between girls and boys and to loud-mouthed attempts to stamp the 'otherness' out of me.

There's a saying that our worst enemy is our best teacher, and there's a sense in which this was true in my case. My experiences in Graz taught me that I was stronger than I thought. Yes, I could be brought to tears by the injustices, hostility and pointless arguments that I faced – but I also had a fighting spirit in me that many underestimated. When it comes to reaching my goals, I can be unbelievably tenacious. At such times I'm like water, finding my way round any wall or obstacle standing in my way even if it means carving out an entirely new path. My goal at the time was to successfully complete fashion school, so leaving was out of the question. When things became unbearable at the boarding house, one phone call to my father would have been enough for him to drive over. I never made that phone call. Instead, I clenched my teeth and thought about something that made me happy, which was above all my classes. We were given lessons in drawing and painting, learning all there was to know about the proportions of the body and the power of colour. We discovered how to go from a rough sketch to a garment of professional quality, and were taught the many possibilities for enhancing and reworking fabric. To help us with life after graduation, we had classes in economics that prepared us for the possibility of self-employment. I still use a lot of what I learnt today, despite ultimately choosing a singing career.

My interest in fashion remains strong: the dress in which I caused such a stir at the Eurovision Song Contest was one I'd designed myself. When I've got five minutes to spare, you'll often find me messing around with a pencil and paper, coming up with new designs. I can feel my mind becoming focused in the process – working on a drawing is like getting a breath of fresh air. Each time I do focus like this, I know I'll be able to tackle the tasks ahead with renewed energy. I've spoken to several renowned designers who like to start each day by coming up with a handful of new ideas, and I'm much the same. What I also took away with me from fashion school was an unerring eye for outstanding craftsmanship. Whenever I go to see Karl Lagerfeld or Jean Paul Gaultier, I can't help flipping the most beautiful garments inside out and inspecting how the seams have been put together. I've always strived for perfection and was fully supported in this by the tutors at fashion school.

At the weekend, if my parents asked me how I was doing in Graz, I would tell them about my classes and about how wonderful they were. I was more reticent when it came to life at the boarding house and the difficulties I faced there. Nevertheless, it was enough for my mother and father to come up with a plan: they offered to pay for me to stay in a little flat, as they'd done for Andi. It was the start of a fresh chapter in my life. My new shelter was in the house of a lady who lived on her own and was renting out some rooms on the ground floor. The one drawback was the distance to fashion school: after struggling up a steep hill, I had to catch a tram from the final stop on the line all the way to the city centre. Everything else was pure bliss. My landlady was the type of woman I still swoon over today: stunningly beautiful, intelligent, and independent-minded – a combination that often results in a lonely existence for a woman, since no man can buck up the courage to speak to her. She had studied to become a dental technician, and made her living by travelling around the country and teaching primary school children how to brush their teeth. If fate had ever sent her over to the children of Bad Mitterndorf, we would definitely have become massive fans of dental hygiene.

I sometimes looked after her dog, an adorable golden retriever, and in return she would give me cooking tips. I don't share my mother's talent for whipping up fantastic meals from whatever ingredients she has to hand, regardless of whether she has one or one thousand mouths to feed. The way I saw it, snipping away at vegetables was a tiresome inconvenience. At times, I would find myself wistfully remembering childhood days of coming home after playing out in the fresh air and simply choosing a dish from the menu. Nowadays, I see things from a different perspective: when I was fifteen, I learnt how to cook, wash, clean, and generally do what you have to do to be able to stand on your own two feet. It made me independent. Today, no-one can fob me off with phrases like 'this is how it's done' – I've been my own master too long for that to work. My parents didn't simply write me a blank cheque: while they helped out with the rent, everything else I paid for myself. At one point I decided I wanted a sofa for my little flat. I already had a desk and an armchair – the sofa would be purely a luxury. Along with two girls from my fashion school, I went to have a look round some furniture shops. The sofa I liked the most cost

€300, a figure well beyond my price range. 'Let's head back', the girls were saying. But I had other ideas.

'There are two ways to react when you don't get what you want,' I told them. 'You can give up and go home, or you can find an alternative.' Even at that age, I wasn't the type of person to become disheartened if I encountered a setback. €300 is too expensive? Then I'll find something for €50. Actually, that was still more than I could really afford – but at least it wasn't more than what I *thought* I should be able to afford. I steered my friends to the children's department, and that's where I saw it: an absolutely magnificent inflatable sofa selling for a joyous €49.99. 'I'll even get change!' I joked as we made our way to the till. The girls started to laugh. 'You always come up with the best ideas – we'd never have thought of looking in the children's section. That sofa's awesome!'

There's a term you sometimes hear today – helicopter parenting – which refers to anxious, over-protective parents who constantly hover over their child, to the extent that the child never develops the ability to do anything independently. That wasn't the way my mother and father treated me. They made me think for myself, instilled in me their values, helped me to be courageous: what's important is that you enjoy what you do, they used to tell me. They wanted me to achieve. So long as my grades were good, they would happily carry on financing my flat, no question about it. Having this simple arrangement in place suited me fine. In fact, we only ever went through one real crisis – and it was triggered by me.

CHAPTER FOUR

COMING OUT

'I want to break free'

FROM THE MUSICAL *WE WILL ROCK YOU*

It was around this time that I started to do the odd gig as a singer, performing mostly at very low-key, informal events. Nevertheless, word began to spread and every now and then I would be asked to give an interview for a radio station, newspaper or magazine. The interviews usually just involved answering a few trivial questions for local media, but one day I found myself sitting across the studio from Anita Ritzl – or Niddl, as she's better known. Niddl had been a contestant on the first series of *Starmania*, a hugely popular talent show screened on Austrian television, where she had reached fourth place. Now she was working for a magazine and had invited me in for an interview. Maybe we'll talk about *Starmania*, I mused. Maybe she's got wind of the fact that I'm thinking of becoming a contestant myself. As it was, we didn't talk about *Starmania* at all. Completely out of the blue, our discussion turned to the question of my homosexuality, something about which I'd never spoken in public. All of a sudden I was being asked: is it true, or isn't it? There I was, seventeen years old, in many ways still a child but an adult nonetheless. This magazine would be read by hundreds of thousands of people, my parents included. And now this question: is it true? Or isn't it? My entire future hinged on that tiny word *it*, that word with which those who are 'normal' define those who are 'abnormal': the word with which heterosexuals define homosexuals, whites define blacks, the able define the disabled, the sighted define the blind. *It* determines whether we belong or are separate, *it* leads to integration or discrimination, *it* is what tells us humans apart.

So, is *it* true?

Or isn't *it*?

From the maelstrom of thoughts racing through my head the following sentence was gradually formed: 'I don't want to lie about this anymore.' About *it*. About who I was. About what I liked, which didn't feel different or strange or whatever else it had been labelled over the previous years. And so I took a deep breath and gave the honest answer: 'Yes, Niddl, *it* is true! Yes, Austria! Yes, Germany! Yes, Switzerland! And Yes! to whoever else happens to read this one day: *it* is true. I am gay.'

They say the truth always comes to light in the end – but did it really have to come to light like this, emerging right into the spotlight? The problem was that 'Yes, Niddl', and 'Yes, readers', also meant: 'Yes, mum and dad, your son is homosexual.' Perhaps you already suspected, perhaps you already knew, perhaps you had been suppressing it – but now he's shouted it out for everyone to hear. He hasn't opened up to you first, like he should have done. Words are tumbling from his lips and it's far too late to try holding them back now. Because he doesn't want to lie anymore. Because he's already been through too much. Because in his deepest heart he believes that the truth has the power to change everything. Holding this belief means being convinced of the good in everyone. It's something I still believe today. And then the interview was over. Niddl had turned off her microphone. One of the assistants gave me a pat on the back and said I'd been 'very brave'.

I knew I'd made the biggest mistake of my life.

CHAPTER FIVE

THE ROAD TO CANOSSA

'What is this feeling, so sudden, and new?'

FROM THE MUSICAL *WICKED*

The magazine was due out four days after the interview. At that point, Bad Mitterndorf would know what Bad Mitterndorf had always suspected: the boy from the local restaurant is gay, is homosexual. Anything might happen then, or at least that's what my overheated imagination was telling me. The locals could turn against us, and my parent's restaurant stand empty. Or worse still: people could start harassing them, just like they'd harassed me. I grew even more anxious when I thought about the lack of trust I'd shown towards my parents. I'd revealed in public what I should have told them in person. The fact that I hadn't planned things that way, that my mouth had – as the saying goes – run away with itself, that one word had led to another: these things were no longer important. I was infinitely sorry about what I'd done, yet there was no way

25

to take it back. Faced with this situation, I picked up the phone and called my grandma.

My grandma is a remarkable woman. Life has by no means been a bed of roses for her – far from it. I remember as a child catching snatches of the conversation between the old men who were regulars at our restaurant. They would talk about the 'bad times' during and after the war. The state of Styria had been occupied by the British, while Burgenland, its eastern neighbour, came under Soviet control. In the early days of the Cold War, everyone lived in constant fear of the Russians mobilising their tanks and extending the boundaries of the Eastern Bloc further westwards. This was the era in which my grandma grew up. She was born into a large family with many siblings, and since money, food and pretty much everything else was in short supply, she became a so-called *holiday child*, spending most of her childhood in Portugal, not far from Lisbon. She was taken in by a wealthy family and came into contact with a whole new way of life. Her foster father ran a chocolate factory, which always made me think of *Charlie and the Chocolate Factory* whenever my grandma mentioned it. She learnt Portuguese in the space of a summer; visited Bairro Alto and Chiado – two of Lisbon's ancient city quarters; went on excursions along the Tagus River; and she was very well taken care of.

'After four o'clock,' she would recall, 'we girls weren't allowed down to the beach anymore. It was when the factory workers finished work for the day, and they didn't always know how to behave themselves.' Everything she saw back then was new to her, yet she never stopped being inquisitive and hungry for knowledge. One time she took me aside and said to me: 'Sea folk are different from mountain folk.' She was talking about the difference between her childhood home in Portugal and her home back in Austria. 'The sea always brings in something new. You soon learn that just because something's different, it doesn't mean it's bad.'

She later returned to Austria, where she eventually met my grandpa. He had jet black hair and a swarthy complexion, as if to prove that, even in the mountains, the unexpected does happen every now and then. He wore gold-rimmed glasses, smoked exotic-smelling cigarettes and earned a living as a long-distance lorry driver. I'm certain that it's from him I inherited the nomadic genes that make me just as keen a traveller as he was. He told me about his journeys all over Europe, about the harbours of Rotterdam and Marseille and the pine trees that lined the streets of northern Sweden. My grandpa transported fridges and televisions, coffee and sugar. Once, on unloading a couple of crates of bananas he'd transported to Antwerp, he discovered hundreds of spiders that had come along for the ride and that presently crawled out of the crates and all over the inside of his truck.

Sadly, he died young, and ever since then my grandma had lived on her own. We went to see her regularly, and the two-hour car journey felt like an eternity to me. Sometimes I dozed off and the first thing I saw on waking up was the big cartwheel that hung in the hallway of her house, telling me we'd finally arrived. I'd charge from the car and jump into my grandma's arms. It always smelt good at her place, a mixture of menthol and eau de cologne. While staying at Karl Lagerfeld's for a recent photoshoot, I had a sense of déjà-vu: it smelled just like my grandma's at his place, and I was immediately transported back to a more carefree existence. No wonder I felt so at ease in his presence – I'm sure my grandma would too. She always kept her place spick and span. There was never a speck of dust on any surface, nor so much as a droplet of water splashed on the sides of the ceramic bath tub. We could have eaten off the floor if it hadn't been bad manners.

Her house was set into a hillside, and life played itself out mainly on the upper floor, in the conservatory and in the garden. In order to bring a little bit of nature into the house, she'd put up a gigantic canvas of a lake surrounded by a forest of fir trees, and had covered the floor in moss-green carpet. There it was again, now for the third time in my life: the Green Cave. It was a sheltered existence I led at my grandma's, though this was also in part because she was a born leader and didn't let anyone make the decisions but herself. She was the one that set the tone in our family, and even though she bossed me around a bit, she was still a calming person to be around. It's from her that I inherited the determination to make up my own mind, although back when I was child I loved letting her be the one in charge.

Perhaps this was what led me to make that desperate phone call and tell her about what I'd just done. It was also the first time I'd talked about my homosexuality with her, but she didn't waste any time discussing it. After all, she'd learnt that just because something's different, it doesn't mean it's bad.

'You're to go home,' she said in a voice that told me it was no use trying to argue. 'And I'll be there soon.'

'But grandma, you'll have to drive for two whole hours, and—'

She didn't even let me finish the sentence. 'It's for the best', she said, and I knew she was right.

I'd always enjoyed travelling back home to my parents, even when there'd been a real danger that someone might be lying in wait for me at the station. This time, however, the journey couldn't go slowly enough. I remembered that there was a term – the 'Walk to Canossa' – that refers to the act of making a humiliating apology. King Henry IV had been forced to go to Canossa after being threatened with excommunication by the Pope. According to the history books, the King had had to wait outside Canossa Castle 'barefoot and until four days had passed' before he was let in. I was sure that my parents weren't going to force me to wait out in the street for four days, yet this didn't stop me feeling like a penitent going to seek forgiveness. It didn't matter that I was already well past the stage of being bothered by my homosexuality. The real issue was that I hadn't given my parents a chance to prepare themselves for this.

My aim was to burst through the front-door, grab hold of them and immediately confront them with the truth – a sort of 'This-is-the-situation-so-deal-with-it' approach. As I'd feared, that day they already had enough going on as it was and were working flat-out preparing meals, setting up the dining room and making up beds for new guests. Now on top of all this here I was, showing up with news that no one had any time for right at that moment. All three of us were overwhelmed by the situation, and I remember an awful argument breaking out. It was a disagreement about the manner in which I'd come out, something it was already too late to change, and by the end of it each us was in tears.

It was at this point that my grandma turned up. I'd already forgotten all about the fact that she was coming. The elegant poise, grace and authority she exuded swept through the room like a spring breeze. Without so much as a 'hello', she launched into commander mode:

'Shouldn't you be sorting things out for when the guests show up this evening?' she asked my parents. 'Pull yourselves together and get to work.'

I spent the next few days at my grandma's house, during which time my parents calmed down a great deal. I got a phone call from my brother, whom I'd already told three years previously that I was gay and whose only response had been: 'Well, it figures.' My parents still needed a little longer to reach the point where it figured. Every so often, they tell me how grateful they are to me for teaching them to care less about what other people think. This always strikes me as remarkable: in our society it's usually meant to work the other way round, with children learning from their parents. The very existence of the concept of 'coming out' – this bizarre term that really just expresses the idea that people are obliged to tell others about what or whom they like – shows how far away we are from being a tolerant society. My mission as Conchita Wurst is to change this.

There's still a long way to go.

CHAPTER SIX

STARMANIA

'Wonder of wonders, miracle of miracles'

FROM THE MUSICAL *FIDDLER ON THE ROOF*

No matter how talented a singer you are, you'll struggle to make it big if the only venues you ever play are your attic and other people's birthday parties.

Although I'd never had the benefit of traditional vocal coaching, it felt like the time was right to start performing in public. Nowadays, I sometimes joke that it was the Little Mermaid who taught me how to sing, though this is obviously stretching things a little. After all, she was busy sacrificing herself for love in the hope of transforming from a mermaid into a human. Looking back today, I realise that I was planning something along the same lines: a transformation so complete and so earth-shattering as to be almost inconceivable. But that was all still to come. Even so, every journey begins with a single step, and I decided to sign up for *Starmania*.

The show had already run for two series and they were

now auditioning for the third. Language is full of sayings such as 'He Who Dares, Wins' and 'If You Don't Ask, You Don't Get'. It doesn't change the fact that it takes real courage to put yourself out there and to ask yourself the question: 'Am I capable of this?' The first two series had attracted a decent number of viewers and the show's producers now wanted to go even further. Arabella Kiesbauer, a TV personality from Vienna who'd risen to fame with her talkshow *Arabella*, would be returning to *Starmania* as the host. There had been 2,500 applicants battling it out for 18 places, so it already felt like an achievement to be proceeding to the next round, and I looked forward to having the summer holidays to prepare myself. The point at which the anxiety really kicked in was when I was subsequently selected to go through to the finals. How are you going to manage this, I began to ask myself: you've got school all day and then homework most evenings. It wasn't clear how I'd find the time to squeeze television shoots into this packed schedule.

If, just as I'm doing now, you spend a few moments looking back at your life, you realise it contains several points where you reached a crossroads: points where you had to make a decision that would change the course of your future. You can ponder endlessly about which is the right path to follow. You can also listen to your intuition, that gut feeling that some people say doesn't exist. It definitely exists in my case, and it had some advice for me now.

'You've got to grab this opportunity with two hands,' my instinct whispered to me. 'You can always go back to school later on.'

This was exactly the argument that the rational side of me

needed to hear, reluctant as it was to let me to drop out of school essentially overnight. At first, I didn't tell anyone about the decision I'd made. The first episode went out on 6 October 2006, with one group of singers performing for the first three weeks and a second group performing from 27 October for another three weeks. The first contestant to take the plunge was Dagmar Hinterer, who had to do her performance on the opening night itself. Each of the following weeks saw a new contestant take to the stage. Six weeks later, we were down to the final line-up and then the game was on again: singing, voting, being chosen to stay on or being voted off. It was the first time I'd ever sung in competition with others, and I had mixed feelings about it.

While it was amazing to be able to sing in front of such a large number of people, whenever anyone else was voted off it was as if I was experiencing the same feelings as they were. I'd grown close to several of the other contestants, and their disappointment was my disappointment. Meanwhile, my family and friends had of course become aware of what was happening – and instead of telling me off for not being at school, they were there to cheer me on! I had no option but to win. By this point, we were already into the new year, and on 26 January 2007, for the very first time in my life, I would be taking part in a finale. Millions of viewers! Voting! Two contestants in tears, but only one crying tears of joy! The trailers tried to build up as much suspense as possible, and in the end it was a choice between Nadine Beiler and me. 'There can be only one,' murmured one of the cameramen in my ear, quoting the tagline from the film *Highlander*.

A lot was at stake – specifically, the offer of a recording

contract, something I'd never even dared to dream of until now. Nadine and I both sang our hearts out, each of us put in the best performance we could, and in the end the audience decided. Tom Neuwirth reached second place. Nadine was the jubilant queen. Four years later, she represented Austria at the 2011 Eurovision Song Contest and came eighteenth. As *Starmania* came to a close, the idea that I too would go on to perform at the Eurovision Song Contest never crossed my mind. At that point, I could happily have gone back to my studies. Yet something deep inside me rebelled against this idea.

As part of *Starmania*, contestants had each been assigned a category of music from which they would perform their own version of a song. My category had been 'Eurovision' and had consisted of a choice of five songs, one of which was 'Everything' by Anna Vissi. In her home country of Greece, Anna is a superstar. I don't know whether it was by coincidence or not, but at some point Anna heard me doing a performance of her song, and after my Eurovision victory she invited me to visit her on the beautiful island of Mykonos. The festivities to celebrate her 40 years of performing were under way, and she greeted me like an old friend. There was singing and dancing, food and laughter. Trying to match her energy could be a life goal in itself. She put on a spectacular three-hour show by day, only to dance from dusk till dawn. A remarkable woman! Although it was only the first time that I'd met her, it felt like we'd already known each other for years.

One night, she invited me for a private dinner, over which she spoke to me about her life. Although we were in an exclusive restaurant, Anna had young men fawning over her all evening, sizing me up with envious glances. I couldn't help but smile to myself: life always follows the same pattern. Here's a woman who attracts men like moths to a flame, but none of them stands a chance. Then I come along – someone who adores women, but isn't attracted to them – and can get a tête-à-tête with the drop of a hat.

By the time I returned home, one thing was certain: I wanted to continue along the path on which I'd set out. I had no idea where it would take me, no map in my pocket, no clear destination in mind, but I'd tasted blood. It's possible that I was guided onwards in my decision by a recollection of my favourite musical, *Wicked: The Untold Story of the Witches of Oz*. It follows the story of the Wicked Witch of the West, a character who's always fascinated me. Now I too would be straying from the straight and narrow. I would be doing so timidly, and with reservations, yet firm in the decision to not return to school. Instead of putting my energy into a third year of fashion studies, I jumped for joy every time the phone rang. It was frequently a call from a magazine, a radio station, a TV company. There was a lot of media interest around the *Starmania* contestants, especially the finalists. I could now be glad that I'd already gone through the process of 'coming out'. I no longer had to hide behind a lie when appearing in public, and this was a huge weight off my shoulders.

CHAPTER SEVEN

TAKE THE STAGE!

'You can't stop the river as it rushes to the sea'

FROM THE MUSICAL *HAIRSPRAY*

Starmania – with its heats, semi-finals and finals, and all the surrounding media hype – kept me on tenterhooks for a whole year. People obviously liked to hear me sing, which was great, because it felt amazing being on stage. I love the different ways you can vary the human voice and the way you can use it to evoke emotion. When speaking, we only use a narrow range of frequencies, which often results in very little feeling coming across in what we say. Time and again, I ask myself what on earth it would be like if we spoke to one another by singing. The vocal range of a professional choir covers about two octaves. The top note in the Queen of the Night's aria in Mozart's *The Magic Flute* is two octaves above middle C, so the aria spans a range of two octaves plus a fifth. If you include the accompanying overtones, it's an additional two or three octaves. It's astounding the range of notes we can produce with little more than our larynx, vocal cords, mouth and throat! Of course, in the case of professional singers, the body also has a role. The body is our natural resonance chamber, and you can separate the wheat from the chaff among singers by the way they manage, or don't manage, to make use of their body. The term *supporting the voice* is used when we work with the diaphragm to make our singing appear effortless.

I can no longer remember precisely when singing became just as important, if not more important, to me as talking. It was probably the day that I felt for the very first time that I could give pleasure to people when I performed music on stage. All this played a part when it came to deciding what my next step would be. I once heard that Hollywood has a cast-iron rule stating that a filmmaker is only as good and successful as their last film. Austria might not be America, but the same rules apply to fame and success in my home country.

There was one record company that saw masses of potential if I carried on singing. Not all the *Starmania* contestants were able to release songs – Nadine Beiler, Gernot Pachernigg, Mario Lang and Eric Papilaya come to mind. But the record company had thought up something special for Thomas Neuwirth from Bad Mitterndorf. The plan was for me to become a member of a boy band, an Austrian version of the Backstreet Boys or Take That. My bandmates would be Martin Zerza, Johannes Palmer and Falco De Jong Luneau, and the group's name, jetzt anders! (be different!), said it all. I wasn't exactly overwhelmed with enthusiasm. Someone in a back room had concocted the plan because boy bands were the 'in' thing, but, as with many similar ideas, it lacked heart and soul. At the time, I was not mature enough to follow my intuition and say 'no' to a project that I didn't think was going to be a success. I was told in no uncertain terms that either we become a boy band or we would not be allowed to perform, and I was desperate to go on stage. So I became a member of jetzt anders! and got a taste of failure.

Looking back now, I'm glad I had this experience. It's never certain whether you'll make it as an artist, and you can only really appreciate success if you've already suffered failure. We sang in German, and our output included the tracks 'This Moment' and 'For Ever and Ever'. Although we were ambitious, things just never really took off. The high point of jetzt anders! was when we played at Paris Hilton's birthday party at the Ischgl winter sports resort. One way or another, every guest at the party seemed to be someone important, and so the band's creators thought this might be our big breakthrough. I wasn't convinced. The illusion that something successful can happen just by chance will always remain an illusion. I believe in ideas that flow from the heart, in hard work, discipline, sustainability and in the ten thousand hours it takes to become good at something. None of this applied to jetzt anders!, so it was hardly surprising when the group disbanded eight months later. We couldn't do our name justice. During the last performance we gave, I remember thinking: we're just the opposite of *Nomen est omen* – true to one's name.

I was now out of a job. Sticking with the Hollywood rule, as a singer you're only as good and successful as your last engagement. All of a sudden, I discovered the dark side of being an artist. No releases or downloads, no concerts or club nights, and no life in the limelight. But I was never one for moping around.

'Looking at things objectively, you haven't even started', I told myself. On *Starmania*, I'd been performing covers of songs that others had already sung. Our band jetzt anders! had been the brainchild of marketing experts who'd thought it could be a success. What was missing from all of this was any personal input from me. Despite facing this temporary setback, my thinking remained positive. 'Go your own way', I told myself. Initially, of course, I was at a loss as to what I should do. Ideas don't appear from thin air just because we're suddenly in need of inspiration. Ideas are much smarter than that. They appear when we no longer believe that they will.

Still, there was one small idea that I was able to turn into reality. I wanted to swap Graz for Vienna. Over the past few months, I'd become familiar with the capital and had learnt to love it. If you've already visited Vienna, no further explanation is necessary. If you haven't been, then it's well worth a trip. But beware! Vienna will present you with an irresistible mix of modern metropolis and historical charm, as bubbly as champagne, as sweet as sugar, but always laced with a dash of bitterness – which, as every gourmet knows, can only add refinement to a dish. And it's not just the daytime I'm referring to. The same is true of the night. I myself am a creature of darkness: I want a sensual, passionate, life-affirming existence. Since that was the kind of life I was after, I got a job with the fashion retailer H&M in order to finance it. With my eye for fashion, I didn't find it hard to advise to customers. At first, it was the appeal of doing something new that attracted me, but before too long the magic started to fade. I began to notice that arranging clothes, putting them back, sorting them, hanging them up, selling them and then passing them nicely packaged over the counter could not be what my life was all about. There was a danger that one day I would still be standing there without any professional qualifications. That's one thing I wanted to avoid at all costs. Still, when I turned my back on H&M and left Vienna, I was sure that this wonderful city would be seeing me again.

To begin with, I went back to Graz and did my third year at the Fashion College, taking up my work with needle and thread just as skilfully as before. This time, though, I had the advantage of being a bit older than the others – and a bit more famous. Perhaps it was that the bullying had stopped, or that my self-confidence had grown: whatever it was, I passed my *matura* – the Austrian school leaving exam – with flying colours and went straight back to Vienna. That was the first cause for celebration. The second was an idea that had hatched at the back of my mind. Like I said, good ideas tend to steal up unsolicited and unannounced. This one felt a little bit strange: it was definitely something different. It also came from the heart, and, as I now know, that's where every good idea begins.

CHAPTER EIGHT

GUAPA, CONCHITA, GUAPA!

'It won't be easy, you'll think it strange
When I try to explain how I feel'

FROM THE MUSICAL *EVITA*

Throughout my life, there had been many occasions where I'd played the game of a man transforming himself into a woman. It had started in my childhood when, every now and then, I would slip into women's clothing. The first time I did this in public was at a carnival event, and I subsequently honed it to perfection during the long hot nights of a Viennese summer. What I actually wanted at the time was to become more muscular and butch, perhaps in order to find recognition, at least on a superficial level, in the gay community. Yet I could eat as much as I wanted – and still can – without putting on an ounce. The classiest women's clothing fitted me like a glove, and so gradually I began to experiment with more and more things: clothes, wigs, makeup, the lascivious game of seduction. I noticed how both men and women got a kick from this really quite narrow area of erotic pleasure. Not being able to avert their eyes any longer, they would boldly ask, 'Are you for real?' It's a dangerous question, because it's not too far off from: 'What's wrong with you? Is that really *you?*' No matter how deeply we explore the human psyche, we always end up with indecision and hesitation when we confront our ego. Who am I? What makes me the person I am? Men in women's clothing, drag queens, often provoke this question, perhaps the most important in life. Legend has it that the term 'drag' was originally coined by William Shakespeare, who noted it alongside his stage directions whenever a man appeared in women's clothing, or dressed as a girl.

When I started to explore drag, I felt as if the concept had been created specially for me. I began to accept my body and enjoyed seeing women get jealous. Where did you get a waist that size? How on earth can you fit into this dress? How do you manage to walk in those heels as if you've done it all your life? If I wore them, I'd end up breaking my neck!

The deeper I delved into this world, the clearer it became to me that the search for one's true self is a life-long quest, like the challenge of learning to love oneself. These thoughts were on my mind when I was invited to a party one evening in Vienna. In response to the call of love, a friend of mine was moving to Hamburg, the German city of vice, of the famous Reeperbahn street of bars and the red light districts of St Pauli and St Georg. The perfect opportunity to get my heels out, I decided. One of my closest friends, Matthias, did my hair, while my wonderful friend Nicole, whom I'd met doing *Starmania*, showed off her skills in the art of verse. She composed a poem that I then did my best to perform in High German [an old German dialect]. Much fun was had by all, and after I'd finished my rendition, one of the guests took me to one side. It was Kitty Willenbruch. I recognised her at once: Kitty and her burlesque-revue show were famous throughout Vienna. She was looking for a compere and thought I might be the right man – or woman – or both – for the job. As a man, I felt comfortable with my beard. It wasn't as immaculate as my beard today, so Matthias touched it up with some makeup just for that evening. It was an idea I'd been toying with for some time: if this is a game in which a man squeezes into a bra, pads it out and then puts on a pair of excruciatingly uncomfortable panties to conceal his manhood – if this is what he does to transform himself into a woman – then why on earth shouldn't he benefit from what nature has given him? And this includes facial hair. When you think about it, the Bible tells us that God made Eve from one of Adam's ribs – so this is a game with a long history behind it.

'Sounds good,' I said to Kitty, and I meant it: it really did *sound* good, which is important for me as a singer.

'What stage name do you want to use?'

It's a question asked not only at leaving parties, but also when you make the decision to turn professional. I shrugged my shoulders, not knowing what to say. 'No idea. I'll have to think about it.'

And that's precisely what my friends did when I told them about Kitty's offer.

'What about Concha?' asked Damavis, who was from Cuba and had a penchant for Spanish-sounding names. 'Guapa Concha, guapa! Beautiful Concha, pretty girl!'

'No, no!' I protested. 'It sounds like a brand of chewing gum. No way!'

This just went to show I wasn't up to the job of being a prophet just yet. Fortunately, Damavis stuck to her guns. 'In Cuba we always refer to the sexiest women as conchas. Or conchitas, if they're really sweet. And you're not telling me you don't look sweet in that get-up, are you?'

I now pricked up my ears. To me, Conchita sounded different, lovelier, sweeter. And my creation really was sexy – I'd already seen the effect she could have on people of either gender. Despite that, I didn't warm to the idea immediately. 'Well, if you think so. Whatever. Probably not worth giving a damn.' (Or, as we say in German, *ist ja auch wurst.*)

And there it was: *wurst.* A word every Austrian understands, because it's a common way of saying you don't give a damn, or couldn't care less. All of a sudden, I remembered how my parents hadn't had the luxury of not giving a damn about what other people thought since their livelihood depended on it, and what impact this attitude had had on my own life. I became aware of the whole variety of senses the word can be used to convey: it's used in expressions that range in meaning from 'what do I care?' to 'I can't afford not to care!'. Such a lot of power for such a small word! The die was cast.

'Conchita Wurst,' I announced. 'That's what I'll call myself.' And so I did.

CHAPTER NINE

THE LETTER

'Know that I was always there'

FROM THE MUSICAL *BILLY ELLIOT*

In 2011, as one friend of mine moved to Hamburg, another needed a compere for her show. As a result, Conchita Wurst was born – at least, that's how things might appear to have happened from the outside. In reality, Conchita had existed inside me for some time, as shown by a letter I wrote her a year later. We don't need to plumb the deepest depths of psychology, but, as I live in the home city of Sigmund Freud, the world-famous father of sexual psychology, allow me to quote his colleague and long-standing friend C. G. Jung, whose basic principles of psychoanalysis can be summarised in the following words: we can't suppress what is inherent within us. If we try to do so, we'll eventually reach breaking point – something we see, hear and read about in the news every day. It's much healthier for us if we address what's inside us and wants to come out. In my case, it was Conchita and what

Conchita stood for: tolerance and love, or everything that can make our world a better place.

Dear Conchy,

It's the late 1990s, and you don't really exist. Little Tom is still hiding you away in his imagination. But you're already there, and the 10-year-old boy knows it. He'll find his own subtle way of giving expression to you by dressing up in women's clothes. Because it's so much fun. You are, to be honest, something of a forbidden fruit at this point in time. Not many of the people who know Tom are happy with his feminine side. But never fear, dear Ms Wurst: your time will come! Tom must first make it through a few difficult years generally known as puberty. This is the time in a boy's life when he grows up and is forced to face annoying things such as his own identity. Believe me, this is never a fun time. That's why you, dear Conchy, will have to stay hidden for a few more years yet. During this time, Tom will learn how to gain personal benefit from negative experiences, through self-reflection and situational analysis. Don't laugh! At his age, he still doesn't know why people give these things such complicated names. But he'll learn to distinguish between others disliking him and hating themselves. 'Do they dislike me because I'm gay? Or do they treat me like this because they can't stand themselves?' These are questions he'll ask himself. We both know, Conchita, that it was mostly the second of the two.

So the years go by, and you still have no proper appearance and no name. But be patient! Your moment of fame will come. After waiting twenty-three years on the bench, you'll suddenly be sent out onto the pitch. With your long black hair and even longer eyelashes, wearing incredibly uncomfortable shoes and sporting a beard. Yes, that's right, love. You'll have a beard. Why? Because no one gives a damn.

In doing so, you'll open up a new reality to an insecure young boy and empower him to lead a life in which he can be what he wants to be and be who he really is. With your help, he'll fight for a bit more tolerance and acceptance. And as far as I, your future ego, can judge these things, you'll endure each other's company for a good while.

With love, Tom

CHAPTER TEN

THE WORLD IS YOUR OYSTER

'Then you begin to make it better'

FROM THE MUSICAL *ALL YOU NEED IS LOVE*

In one of his interviews, John Lennon recalled the time before The Beatles made it to world stardom. Between 1960 and 1962, they gave a record number of 270 concerts, some of which lasted six, eight or even ten hours. The concerts took place in a strip club on Hamburg's Reeperbahn, where a nightclub owner by the name of Bruno had brought in nonstop striptease. The Beatles played to attract passers-by, and John Lennon commented on these formative years of the cult band as follows: 'We played the whole night. We had to work flat out and come up with new ideas all the time. That made us widen our repertoire, get better and gain in self-confidence.'

I went through a similar process on becoming a compere at Kitty's revue show in Vienna. Her revue was a non-stop underground show performed in front of a discerning public who wouldn't allow themselves to be fobbed off with cheap ideas. We were socially critical, with our finger on the pulse: when we tore a politician to shreds, we sometimes knew more than the next day's papers. Just like The Beatles on the Reeperbahn, we worked flat out, constantly coming up with new ideas, and this helped to broaden my horizons. I got better and better, Conchita got better and, most importantly, I got to know her better.

To begin with, I gave her a social context, a back-story, as they call it in the filmmaking world. So Conchita first sees the light of day in the Colombian highlands, where she was married to Jacques Patriaque, played by my talented friend Thomas. This gave us an opportunity for an on-stage dialogue, ranging from biting short sketches to full-length plays. Our stage setting was reminiscent of the 1920s, when Vienna vied with Berlin for the title of hub of European culture. In New York, we would have been classed as off-Broadway or off-off-Broadway. Similarly, in Vienna, the city of opera, operetta and Austrian national theatre, we were initially just part of the underground scene. That's where news about us began to spread. First, the established arts scene made quiet references to Salon Kitty Revue. Next, the first visitors turned up, curious to see for themselves what was behind the whispered recommendations. There was talk of a woman with a beard and her seductive husband, really hot stuff. Not wishing to miss out, more and more people started turning up at our shows. Until that point, I'd always borrowed my high heels, but it was now worth my while going to the right shops and buying my own. I started looking for wigs and discovered how much technology went

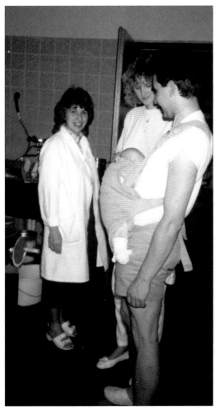

Below left: Even with a newborn, you still have to mind the shop. While I was strapped onto my father's belly it fell to my mother to look after the guests at the youth hostel in Ebensee.

Below right: Occasionally my grandmother would come to visit us, which was always a special occasion.

On Sunday my parents liked to go on little day-trips with me and my brother Andreas.

Above left: My guinea pig Bob and I in our garden in Bad Mitterndorf. Our favourite game was 'catch', Bob haring off and me chasing behind.

Above right: A group picture with a rocking horse: My cousin Alexander, my cousins Birgit and Christa, my brother Andreas and I are beaming with joy.

Below: At my First Communion I was far more fascinated by the dress my best friend Kristin was wearing than anything to do with the ceremony. I probably thought I should have a beautiful one just like it.

Right: Our Trio Infernale. I performed alongside Jacques Patriaque and Urinella on stage at Kitty Willenbruch's burlesque revue. Jacques played my husband, while Urinella was the grande dame who wore her heart on her sleeve. We displayed razor-sharp wit, and we knew how to party – we still do!

Above left: At the Halloween party at the U4 club in Vienna: it wasn't Prada the devil wore, but Versace. Donatella had turned up, and she was most definitely not amused. Anyone who spoke to her was sent packing in no uncertain terms. And anyone looking to dance with her only got to see her claws. So there was much laughter when it was later revealed that Donatella was me. No-one had recognised me, they'd all thought I was the real thing.

Below right: It's mid-May and it's time for the Vienna Life Ball. Despite the thermometer showing just 8°C, I'm still skimpily dressed. But that didn't dampen the mood, either on or off stage.

Above left: At fashion school in Graz, I learnt how to design clothes and do dressmaking. I'm still passionate about designing my own things, including the dress I wore at the Eurovision Song Contest, but nowadays I rarely get an opportunity to pick up the needle and thread myself. So when my friend Nicole was getting married, I seized on the chance to get my sewing machine running flat-out again. This three-layered circle skirt à la Swinging Fifties needed a lot of material. It was great fun!

Middle left: The immediate effect, however, was that I felt pretty shattered after my long day at *Die große Chance*. So here I am enjoying an after-work drink in Café Blaustern.

Below right: MuTh in Vienna is a special place. It's the concert hall of the Vienna Boys' Choir, and it's got a superbly equipped stage, which is said to have the best acoustics in the city. It's a place where you can experience not just the Vienna Boys' Choir, but also rock and jazz concerts. Even Conchita has appeared there. But not this time round, because it was New Year's Eve. At the time this photo was taken, we were just hours away from the magic year that was to be 2014. Me surrounded by my friends: what could be nicer? From right to left: Nicole, Karin, Hannah, Matthias and Anja.

Top left: One of the most exciting taxi rides of my life. I was on my way to the talent show *Die große Chance*, where I sang 'And I Am Telling You I'm Not Going' and 'My Heart Will Go On'. I made it to the final, after which things were never quite the same again.

Middle right: Do you really need to get dressed up like that to go to Africa? Yes, you do, when it's the TV broadcaster RTL asking you to take part in *Wild Girls: An Adventure in Namibia, Home to the Himba Tribe*. Not only did I walk through the desert sand in high heels, I also had a fantastic time.

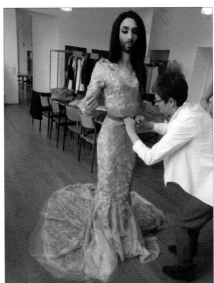

Above left: Patricia Kaas, the great French singer, received me backstage in her dressing gown. Having told me how she herself had competed in the 2009 Eurovision Song Contest in Moscow, she was keen to hear my take on things.

Above right: Trying on my dress for the Eurovision Song Contest finals. I designed it, but it was made by ART for ART in Vienna. I was so lucky to find people with the expert skills needed for my design: white glitter-speckled tulle, overlaid with golden spangles and Swarovski crystals, all sewn on by hand. The overall effect was to give an impression of stardust. On top of that, there was the three-metre-long train: no wonder I was dubbed 'Queen of Europe' after my victory.

Below: It was raining red roses – a dream come true for my first ever solo video. Being showered with petals was a wonderful feeling. We needed to work at speed, though, as rose petals don't stay fresh for long in the heat of the spotlights.

Above left: Ahead of the Eurovision Song Contest, I went on a European tour, travelling through a dozen countries, giving over 400 interviews and being constantly filmed – such as here in Amsterdam, one of my favourite European cities.

Above right: One of the many nice things about the Eurovision Song Contest is that each competing artist gets to create a special version of their national flag. Iceland cut theirs from blocks of ice, while the Dutch used tulips. With the help of my friend Tamara, I made a flag from ball gowns. We shot the clip at Schönbrunn Palace Theatre, which was built on the instructions of Empress Maria Theresa in 1745. It was baroque as far as the eye could see – perhaps that's why Tamara couldn't stop laughing?

Middle left: I once read that one clown is worth more than forty doctors. I know the value of laughter from my own experience. This was especially true in the hours before the Eurovision Song Contest finals. We'd worked hard, rehearsed a lot and done everything we could to deliver the perfect performance on the night. Then someone came up with the idea of taking this photo. René, Matthias, Nicole, Tamara and me, laughing our heads off as we're on a ride at the Prater fun fair in Vienna. We couldn't control ourselves, and it definitely made everything feel easier afterwards.

Below: It was such an emotional experience looking at the points board during the Eurovision Song Contest. A total of thirteen times, I was awarded the maximum '… and twelve points go to Austria'. In the end, I won with 290 points, the fourth-highest score of all time.

Above: Home at last! I've got no idea how long I was on my feet or when I'd last grabbed a few hours' sleep. But then the door of my apartment closed behind me, I took the trophy in my hand again, and posted this photo. After that I went to bed. I slept and slept and slept. And when I finally woke up, the trophy was still there. So it can't all have been a dream!

Above: The Austrian delegation at the Eurovision Song Contest. When I said it was not just a victory for me, but a victory for everyone who believes in a future that's free from discrimination and is based on tolerance and respect, I could be sure I was speaking for all these wonderful people.

Top: At the Life Ball in Vienna, soon after the Contest. It was my first major outing after the ESC finals. Together with Jean Paul Gaultier, I took to the magenta (not red!) carpet. There was time for a quick kiss, and then came the moment when my friend Julian Laidig shot one of my favourite photos. With chaos breaking out all around me, I still seem quite unconcerned. Julian managed to capture this wonderful moment for eternity. Even better, he managed to capture eternity itself.

Below: Fashion designer Vivienne Westwood is a visionary. We chatted like best friends at the Vienna Life Ball. I was captivated by her British sense of humour – and by her perfume, a marvellous mixture of menthol and eau de Cologne, which took me back to my childhood.

Top: Here I am working with Julian Laidig again. As my dress is too short, the stylist has to lengthen it a little. No doubt about it, a photo shoot requires everything you've got!

Above right: Here they are, the winning team from Copenhagen! Tom Reinberger, Monika Ballwein, René Berto, Nicole Fernández-Fernández, Matthias Steurer. And there's me in the middle. Tamara Mascara isn't there. Where were you, Tamara?

Above left: It was something both of us had looked forward to: here's Austrian President Heinz Fischer and me during the TV recording for *Light into Darkness*. The year after, I went on to win the Eurovision Song Contest, while the President celebrated his tenth year in office.

Below right: My parents and grandmother were with me when I went to the Federal Chancellery. The atmosphere was surprisingly relaxed, and we shared a lot of laughs. When it comes to politics it seems like people think you must always be very serious. In my opinion, we can always do with a bit more humour.

Above left: Gery Keszler is the brilliant organiser of the Life Ball in Vienna, Europe's biggest charity event in support of those suffering with HIV and Aids. Every year, it attracts stars such as Bill Clinton, Sharon Stone, Elton John and Catherine Deneuve. Staged in the area around Vienna Town Hall, the event is a marvellous mix of show, ball and revue. And a place where you're sure to come across Conchita – so book now!

Middle right: Carine Roitfeld spent ten years as chief editor at the French *Vogue*, the world's leading fashion magazine. For her *CR Fashion* Book, she had me photographed by Karl Lagerfeld – photos that Carine called 'The New Normal', though they were anything but.

Below left: With Gery Keszler, Rosario Dawson and co. at the amfAR Gala in Cannes. At this point we're still standing in the park of the Hôtel du Cap-Eden-Roc. Just a few moments later, we were sprinting across the lawn. Then across fields. Then climbing over rocks. We finally reached the cliffs above the sea, where there was a fantastic view. Unfortunately, no-one took a shot of it.

Above: Anna Vissi is a superstar in her native Greece. She invited me to the fortieth anniversary of her stage debut on Mykonos and after giving a fantastic three-hour show during the day, she still danced from dusk till dawn.

Below: When it comes to hair, getting it right can take time. Fortunately, Jean Paul Gaultier is a man who knows what he wants, and he's got the best makeup artists, such as Odile Gilbert, working for him. And even more fortunately, I've got the patience of an angel. Well… not quite. To be honest, I'm the most impatient person in the world – which really doesn't help in these types of situation.

Top: Jean Paul Gaultier calls me his 'young empress', and that's exactly what I felt like on this evening. At the gala dinner hosted by the French magazine *Vogue*, I got to know Konstantinos Katalakinos, who quipped that being Jean Paul's boyfriend was work enough.

Below left: I took to the catwalk for Jean Paul Gaultier's Haute Couture Show at the Fashion Days in Paris. It was exciting to be given my own comp card.

Below right: I had just jumped out of the taxi and entered into House Gaultier and I was ready to discuss my appearance on the catwalk that afternoon with Jean Paul.

Top: On *The One Show* in London. They've got such beautiful green sofas at the BBC, which reminded me of the Green Cave. Alex Jones was amazed at how good my English was. As for me, I was amazed to meet one of my favourite singers: Sophie Ellis-Bextor.

Inset: 'Congratulations, we love you, Elton & David.' I was so thrilled to receive this recognition from Sir Elton John and his partner David Furnish. And they even sent me orchids, which are one of my favourite flowers.

Below: Backstage at the Bjorn Borg fashion show in Stockholm. That day I was fortunate enough to be able to sit on the front row as the guest of honour.

into their professional manufacture, and how this was an art mastered by only a handful of people. I soon learnt how to apply my makeup to a professional standard and proudly posted the results on Facebook. As my fan base slowly began to grow on social media, people in the outside world started talking more and more about Conchita Wurst. This led to a decisive step forwards: Conchita emerged from the world of shadow, burlesque and creatures of the night and came into the public gaze. *Die Große Chance* was the name of a talent show on Austrian TV, similar to the UK's *Britain's Got Talent*.

It wasn't easy for me, as I had my doubts about appearing on another talent show. While programmes of this kind are a law unto themselves, what they have in common is that they're on the lookout for something original and unique. I thought that was a box I could tick. In the end, however, I only came sixth in *Die Große Chance*, which really doesn't sound like a stunning success, at least not if another famous Austrian, Arnold Schwarzenegger, is to be believed. Like me, he hails from the Austrian province of Styria, and says of himself: 'I only ever wanted to be first, because no one is interested in who comes second.' So who on earth might be interested in someone who came sixth? It had to be someone with vision, someone capable of turning that vision into a reality, and that's how I got to know René Berto.

In interviews, I'm often asked what I think about this or that footballer, football being the sport of the masses. At that point, I usually have to pass, because there's little to connect me and football. Yet there's one comparison I can make: whereas I had so far indulged my pleasure of disguise and burlesque more or less as an amateur, like a child going for a kick-about with his mates on a football pitch, my life now reached a professional turning point, and this was in part down to René Berto. René had long been involved in the arts scene with his agency Genie und Wahnsinn. Several years earlier, he'd entered one of his artists in the Eurovision Song Contest in Riga. He saw in me more than others could see, even more than I myself could see at that point in time. This was down not just to his experience and desire to think outside the box, but also to his ability to ask the right questions: 'What do you want to be? Where do you see yourself in ten years' time? What's your goal?'

What's your goal? If 'Who am I?' is the hardest question of them all, then 'What's your goal?' comes a close second. When I put the same question to other people, they often grow silent. I was no different. Perhaps it's not true that most people don't know what their goal is. Perhaps they simply don't know how to put it into words. The same was true of me. To begin with, hardly anything came to mind. It takes a mentor like René, who's capable of drawing out ideas, to identify someone's goals and the best way to achieve them. His great talent is that he doesn't confuse his own goals with those of his protégé.

Our conversations gradually became more and more in-depth and revelatory. René would ask questions, I would have a think, and, slowly, a memory would work its way to the surface of my consciousness. What was it like, many years ago, when I first realised I had to leave Bad Mitterndorf? I'd decided to pursue a career in fashion, something that was impossible in my home town. Despite being understandably worried, my parents encouraged me to set out for pastures new, and that's what I did, full of apprehension, yet also full of enthusiasm to go out and discover the world – the world that stretches out at our feet, that belongs to us. The world is your oyster.

'That's my goal,' I told René. 'I want to discover the world. I want to conquer it, with everything I've got, and with everything I am. I want to be a world star.'

Those really aren't words that trip lightly off the tongue. After all, there are critics out there who are ready to shoot you down, ready to dismiss such aspirations as arrogant, over the top, brazen, cheeky and big-headed. Even the critic inside your own head won't hold back. You, a world star? Get real! One thing at a time.

Things were different with René. He took it just as seriously as if I'd said I fancied doing a short concert tour of Styria. What he was really after was to find out what I wanted. He sees himself as a strategist who finds the means with which to turn a vision into reality. So we also got to talking about who my role models were. Despite having no real idols, I could and still do get passionate about artists such as Céline Dion, Tina Turner and Cher. None of them came into this world on a bed of roses and they all went through the occasional rough patch. But they nonetheless always remained true to themselves and their artistry. They're personalities, they have what it takes to send shivers of excitement down my spine: a really great singing voice.

I didn't see René for a few days, but then he resurfaced. He brought with him a document that made me go weak at the knees as I read what was written at the top. It was what I'd been talking and dreaming about, what my goal was. When you see something in black and white, it immediately looks much more important and slightly closer to reality than the abstract thought of it. All of a sudden I felt this excitement, the excitement that comes over you when you've found the path to where you're going.

'I wrote this for you,' said René, handing me the document.

I read aloud: 'From talent show to world star.' I read the rest quietly to myself. What was written there had been cleverly thought through. What was written there would change my life. What was written there sounded like a lot of hard work and more discipline than I'd ever exerted. It didn't sound as if success was going to be handed to me on a plate. I thought of my parents, who'd worked hard all their lives, and I thought of my grandparents, who'd done the same. They'd been long-distance lorry drivers, youth hostel managers and restaurant owners; me, I was an artist. Other than that, there wasn't so much difference. If you want to get to the top, you have to get up early. I was in possession of a working alarm clock. So what could go wrong? I smiled and stretched out my hand.

'It's a deal,' I said.

We shook on it.

CHAPTER ELEVEN

MEETING THE HIMBA

'Don't dream it – be it!'

FROM THE MUSICAL *THE ROCKY HORROR SHOW*

Stories have always interested me, as has the art of writing stories. I once came across *The Hero with a Thousand Faces*, a book in which the American author Joseph Campbell describes myths and folk legends from all over the world and draws on them to create a sort of instruction manual for how to tell a story. One of my favourite fairy tales, *The Little Mermaid* by Hans Christian Andersen, fits wonderfully into the template that Campbell puts forward. Through stories she hears from her grandmother, the Little Mermaid learns about the world of humans and decides to go there herself. She has to overcome many obstacles on the way, facing challenges which little by little bring her closer to her real self. When today I ask myself the question 'Who am I?', I know deep down that, by meeting the challenges life throws my way, I'm moving gradually closer to the answer.

As the Little Mermaid discovers, these challenges are often tests on which we don't perform quite as well as we'd hoped. Conchita has had countless such experiences, too. René and I embarked on our adventure full of enthusiasm, sometimes succeeding and sometimes not. There were times when I was at my wits' end wondering how I was going to pay the bills. Then weeks and months would go by during which I would have had to clone myself in order to meet all the requests coming my way. No sooner had I got used to everything being hectic than it seemed we were back at square one again. I sometimes wondered if we were getting closer to our goal or moving away from it. Campbell has a name for this rollercoaster of feelings experienced by everyone setting out on an adventure: *the road of trials*. We battle on, having to negotiate all sorts of tests that we can either pass or fail. Failure always involves an element of giving up. Around this time, it became ever clearer to me that I would never give up on something that came from deep within my heart – and that was where Conchita had come from. This still holds true when I'm confronted with animosity from others today. Faced with that situation, I just think to myself, 'There you go, another test for you. You'll be stronger for it afterwards, and closer to finding the answer to the most important question there is: Who am I?'

It was around this time that I got a special phonecall. The TV broadcaster RTL was on the line, and what they had to offer me was something called *Wild Girls: Across Africa in High Heels*. The idea was that I would stumble my way through the deserts of Namibia as a 'wild girl', part of a pack that included the models and actresses Sara Kulka, Fiona Erdmann and Kader Loth.

As a rule, broadcasters take their show ideas seriously. It isn't a case of making allowances to make life easy for the contestants. When I asked where the show would be located – in the country's capital of Windhoek, perhaps? – I was told: 'No, we're going to Damaraland and then further on towards Kaokoveld, the land of the Himba people.' By this point it was definitely time for me to dig out my old geography textbook.

I didn't know much about Africa, but what I read fascinated me: 200 million years ago, Africa was at the heart of the Pangaea supercontinent. By virtue of its centrality, the African land mass had escaped destruction when Pangaea broke up into pieces, becoming the earth's oldest and most stable continent. That's why the world's oldest forms of life originated there, and also, over a hundred thousand years ago, the human race. The animal and plant worlds were able to evolve almost undisturbed, and today Africa possesses a wealth of 121 diverse ecoregions: rain forests, savannahs and deserts. It was a desert that the programme's producers had sought out for us. The name 'Namibia' was already a hint. It stems from the word 'Namib', the name of the world's oldest desert. 'Namib' actually means 'empty space' or 'place where there is nothing'. Damaraland, on the other hand, is a rocky desert region stretching north from Walvis Bay up as far as Angola – right up to Kaokoveld, the home of the Himba.

This was all fascinating to me. Some of the world's oldest peoples still live in Namibia: the San bushmen, for example, who probably already lived in southern Africa 25,000 years ago; and the Himba, the country's last semi-nomadic people. It seemed obvious that this was not a place to be walking around in high heels. But, then again: how often are you offered the chance to explore one of the oldest parts of the world? So I agreed.

Flying from Vienna to Windhoek, you only need to set your watch back one hour. The ancient continent lies along similar lines of longitude as Europe, which thankfully also rules out jet lag. As soon as we arrived, we started to head north, our car journey taking us through the famous empty space. Every so often, a farm would appear on the horizon, some of them so large that they could easily have swallowed up the whole of Vienna. But it was the colours I found most impressive. Under a steely blue sky, stretching out as far as the eye could see, was an ochre brown landscape, broken up here and there by jet-black rock formations, as if some giants had just abandoned their game of marbles. Swaying in the wind was yellow desert grass on which herds of kudu antelopes were grazing, tended by shepherds from the Herero tribe.

We made good progress along the tarmac roads, which took us as far as Omaruru – but then we hit the notorious washboard roads, so named for their rippled surface of stones and sand. These ripples are capable of rupturing shock absorbers, and made for an incredibly bumpy ride. North of Otjiwarongo, most of the washboard roads came to an end, and we carried on cross-country before finally reaching the place that the television producers had selected. Our job as contestants – and it's always the same for shows of this kind – was to complete various tasks thought up by a couple of crafty-minded writers. People could then vote us out of the game or choose to keep us in. Predictably, constant attempts were made to stoke up artificial conflicts, in the hope of adding some dynamics to the whole escapade. This is not my scene at all. We have enough conflict in the world without having to inflame the situation with artificially induced – and therefore totally pointless – disputes and quarrels. Conchita stands for love and tolerance, and I soon took it upon myself to act as adjudicator and mediator in these disputes. We were frequently joined in our tasks by the Himba, who probably laughed their heads off in secret after witnessing the chaotic ructions staged by the sweaty white people in the middle of the desert. I loved the elaborately-braided hair of the Himba women, and their skin with its reddish glow.

For one of the tasks, three of us wild girls had to keep a fire going all night. Before long, my two fellow contestants had fallen asleep, but I had fun gathering and piling up the material to get a small but steady camp fire going. An African night in one of the most remote corners of our planet is pure magic. As the night went on, the deep black colour of the horizon began to fade into dark blue. The billions of stars in the Milky Way gave one last burst of light before gradually dying away. I continued to hear the noises of prowling animals, as well as the sound of the wind driving the sand along the ground to form more and more dunes. I stood upright by the fire, as I've perhaps stood in some other long-lost time and place, and turned my face to the east. A weak light was beginning to show on the horizon, a tinge of orange shot through the blueness, and then it all happened very quickly: an orb of light pushed its way majestically over the border that for thousands of years marked the end of the world, a place that could never be reached. All of a sudden, the light became so bright that I had to turn away. It was like the raising of a curtain, a curtain that revealed a new day, a new life, a new love and a new existence. Never before had I felt so deeply that anything is possible if you really want it.

Behind me, I could hear groaning as my fellow contestants blearily opened their eyes to see it was daylight.

'Is it morning?' they asked.

I was able to confirm this.

'And is the fire still burning?'

Another yes.

'I'm aching all over. Oh my God, I can hardly move.'

I helped the wild girls to their feet. Anything is possible if you really want it. All the same, I'd had enough of running through the desert in high heels just for the television screens back home. When I was voted off the show shortly afterwards, I had already experienced the most beautiful thing: this moment of magic which has forever awakened in me the dream of Africa, the cradle of the human race.

CHAPTER TWELVE

TOUR DE FORCE

'That's it! What an idea!'

FROM THE MUSICAL *NINE*

When I arrived home, René had a surprise suggestion waiting for me: I ought to compete in the Eurovision Song Contest. Knowing him, I could be sure he'd already have thought this through and lined up some convincing arguments.

'Do you want to take to the stage? Do you want to sing in front of the whole world?' This was a rhetorical question, because we already knew the answer. Of course I did! For me, singing is a lot more than just making music. I feel a great affinity with harmony, which has been part of our musical tradition ever since Johann Sebastian Bach. In bestowing us with *The Well-Tempered Clavier*, this remarkable composer and musician opened up a whole new approach to music, creating the possibility of playing in every key. I'm often overcome when I hear music in its purest form: when we sing a note, such as standard pitch 'A', sounds are produced at different frequencies. Our ears do not perceive these individual sounds, only the combined note – in this case, the A. Yet the individual sounds can be represented using a frequency meter and a computer. What we then see is something truly breathtaking: between all the individual sounds exist swathes of empty space where no sound is being made at all. Music is, above all, silence.

When I get up in the morning and do my first vocal exercises, I can feel this silence. Without it, there'd be no music, something the brilliant composers and musicians who worked in my hometown of Vienna were well aware of. Mozart, Haydn, Schubert, Liszt, Richard Strauss, Gustav Mahler: their symphonies, operas and chamber music provide us with constant proof of this fact.

René's words cut through my reveries: 'And you're sure you understand what this will involve?' Once again, my answer was 'yes'. After all, we'd already done this before. In the preliminary heats for the 2012 Eurovision Song Contest, the band Trackshittaz had narrowly beaten us to represent Austria in Baku. As it turned out, they failed to make it beyond the semi-finals, where they gained just eight points and came last out of 18 contestants. This time we wanted to do better. René had spoken to the organisers at ORF (the Austrian Broadcasting Corporation), who were thinking of throwing in the towel on account of the numerous Eurovision flops our country had suffered. In 1966, the now late Udo Jürgens had won the contest for Austria with his song *Merci, Chérie*. A full 48 years had elapsed since then. There were many people who no longer believed that another victory was possible. It was René who convinced them to try again. Convincing people who are thinking of giving up to change their minds is no trivial matter. In my case, no arm-twisting was needed: I was already raring to go. I knew what awaited me – a gruelling tour across Europe to prepare for the contest – but in exchange I would be allowed to sing. I could hardly wait.

'When do we start?' I wanted to know.

'You can already guess', replied René, unable to keep back a smile. 'Now. Right now.'

And that's what happened. We set to work straight away.

With a population of roughly 740 million, the continent of Europe stretches from the Atlantic coast of Portugal to the Urals and from the North Cape to Cyprus. More than one-fifth of these people watch the Eurovision Song Contest on TV, an incredibly large number! It is hard to think of an event that crosses so many borders and brings together as many people as this contest. We wanted to do the event justice and prepare viewers for the arrival of Conchita Wurst. All of a sudden, my life revolved around airports, planes, trains, taxis, hotels, TV shows – and giving performances. I might fly to Madrid on a Thursday for a *Euroschlager* show, take a six-hour flight to Riga to perform there the next day, and then travel on to Amsterdam to sing on a TV show in Hilversum a day later. Over the course of these few months, I gave over 400 interviews all over Europe and talked about what it was that Conchita Wurst stood for: love, acceptance and enjoyment of the world's universal language, music.

Throughout my travels, I could feel in every bone of my body that I was a child of Europe, of this breathtakingly beautiful – but all too often blood-stained – continent where history can be soaked up with every breath: from the Europe that saw the sophistication of the ancient Greeks to the Europe of the Roman Empire, whose citizens enjoyed a quality of life that would not be matched again for centuries. The Europe of Charlemagne, King of the Franks, who was arguably the founding father of Europe, and was also known as *pater Europae*. But this is also the Europe of empires and battles, of the Thirty Years' War and all the death and destruction it caused, and the Europe of the First and Second World Wars, which resulted in unimaginable suffering throughout the world. Nevertheless, it's the Europe of the great thinkers, of the Enlightenment, of tolerance and respect for human dignity. Equality, brotherhood, freedom – we are also indebted to Europe for these.

When I was born, Europe was split in two by the Iron Curtain. When I was one year old, the Berlin Wall came down, the Soviet Union and the Warsaw Pact fell apart and East and West came closer together. Nowadays, we live in a society of which millions of our ancestors could only have dreamt. During my travels across the continent, I barely ever had to show any ID to be able to go from one country to another. I paid for my coffee in a single currency and could converse with most people in a common language. These achievements are so huge that they sometimes seem trivial, a realisation which awoke in me a new sense of concern for Europe. My tour not only served its real purpose, that of preparing me to take part in the Eurovision Song Contest: it also opened my eyes to the fascinating issue of our shared European homeland. I listened closely wherever I went, talking to people about their wishes and dreams, their worries and woes. My aim wasn't to then go out on the rooftops and shout about what I'd learnt, but sooner or later I started being asked questions myself, and I wasn't afraid to share my views: I love the wonderfully different cultures that make up our continent , and the unique opportunity Europe offers to experience them all side by side. That's why I talked about democracy: without democracy, we couldn't have this variety of cultures, and I believe it's the best political system that exists. That's not to say that democracy isn't complicated at times – of course it is. What's more, it demands active participation. Yet if you share my desire not to be ruled by others, but to shape your own life, the European ideal offers you everything you could ever wish for.

It was with these impressions and thoughts in my mind that I headed back home in early April 2014, having concluded my tour in London. The grand finale of my journey had been the Eurovision Preview Party, which had been held in the Café de Paris, right in the middle of the West End, my favourite part of the British capital. I now had several engagements at home, including a TV show in Vienna that was aptly titled *Welcome Austria*. Austria was giving me one final welcome before seeing me off again in a few days' time. Then it would be 'Welcome to Denmark – Velkommen til Danmark', and we would discover whether I was able to convey my enthusiasm for Europe in music as well in words. This prospect filled me with an excitement that seemed to know no limit: it felt like anything could happen in Denmark.

CHAPTER THIRTEEN

THE NUMBER 11

'I want to make magic,
I want to breathe fire on the stage!'
FROM THE MUSICAL *FAME*

I love the city of Copenhagen, with its tolerant and cosmopolitan citizens. As soon as we landed at Kastrup airport, I felt calm and carefree – not at all as if the toughest time of my life was about to kick off. Copenhagen is a place of light and water and air, and for a few brief moments I forgot that I would be spending most of the next few days shut up indoors. For a fleeting instant, I wondered if it was really right to present music in the form of a competition. After all, music is something that binds people together, not something that divides them. Then I recalled the old European tradition of singers competing against one another, which stretches as far back as the famed thirteenth century Wartburg minstrel contest.

The airport arrivals hall was teeming with cameramen,

journalists and radio reporters. 'Quite nice, really', I thought, 'that a music contest is capable of causing such a buzz. No war, no arguments, no natural or manmade disasters: just a couple of dozen singers performing their songs.' I went to stand in front of the first camera, speaking into a dozen microphones. This is how I spent much of the next few days.

Obviously, we were all feverishly looking forward to the semi-finals. By 'we', I mean the team of people supporting me, who performed their jobs with such dedication that I occasionally suspected they could read my thoughts and wishes. Perhaps this stemmed from the fact that we already knew each other so well, along with the fact that we really *were* a team, in the sense of a close-knit and committed group of people. In addition to René Berto, there was Nicole Fernández-Fernández, Tamara Mascara and Matthias Steurer. They were all anxious to make life behind the scenes as pleasant as possible for me. The B&W Hall on the island of Refshaleøen was really something: the stage was huge, and sorting out the lighting posed some difficulty. I was dying to meet the other contestants, especially Aram Sargsyan – a.k.a. Aram Mp3 – who was representing Armenia. Hugely popular in his homeland, he was one of the favourites to win.

Then there was Swedish singer Sanna Nielsen, who had sparked my interest by citing Céline Dion as one of her inspirations. I completely agree: I think Céline is a stellar singer. In fact, in a neat coincidence, she won the Song Contest the same year as I was born. Like many other people, I had barely heard of Dutch duo Ilse DeLange and

Waylon, probably because I rarely listen to country music. There were many acts that were in with a strong chance, and there was a lot of lively discussion among the experts as to who would ultimately be the winner, which I thought was great. There's nothing more boring than a contest where the winner is a foregone conclusion. What was key for me was that Europe stood at the centre of things, with every spectator able to see how colourful and unique our shared homeland is. Subsequent newspaper reports spoke of a show that offered 'something for everyone'. Even today, I think there's something truly impressive about the idea of Eurovision as proof that we're not wasting our time trying to make everything look the same. Instead, we're celebrating cultural diversity. In a sense, it felt like it was already a victory just to be involved in that celebration – though obviously there was a part of me that wanted to win.

Today, if I try to recall the last few minutes before going on stage, I find that the events in my hotel room of the previous night superimpose themselves on my thoughts. As I stood in front of the mirror, pondering what I could say if I won, I reflected on my past, on where I had come from, and on how I came to reach this point. I thought about little Tom, from his quiet little corner of Europe; and also about the elegant Conchita, and how she embodies the rising from the ashes, the birth of a new ideal. And then I started to think about the number 11. It wasn't so much from a mathematical perspective, where 11 is the smallest two-digit prime number. In astrology, the number 11 represents incompleteness. This was something that resonated with me, as Tom had also been incomplete until Conchita stepped into his life. The number 11 seemed to have been springing up all over the place recently. My birthday is in the eleventh month of the year, and 11 was also the number of my hotel room, as well as my number in the running order for the final. What's more, the number 11 would frequently crop up in my calculations whenever I had to work anything out in my head. We returned home from the contest on 11 May, touching down at 11:16 a.m. It was only the rainbows over the B&W Hall on the day of the final that came in pairs – eleven rainbows would no doubt have been too much of a good thing. While I'm not someone who's constantly trying to read a deeper meaning into things, there was something about all this that made me feel excited. It generated a positive feeling inside me, which is known to act as a source of previously untapped energy. People say that 'faith can move mountains'. By this they mean that possessing a positive inner attitude can shape what happens in reality. It's up to you whether you believe in this or not, but that night before the final, as I marvelled at the frequency of the number 11, a second scene arose in front of me. In the first one I had been little Tom, but now I was Conchita, standing on the stage in front of thousands of spectators, victorious. Whenever such visions appear, we quickly push them aside – we don't want to see what can't possibly happen, and in pushing them aside, we are also shaping reality. This vision was one that I didn't cast away. Instead, I stayed with it for a good five minutes – a very long time when it comes to visions.

Did I go to bed afterwards feeling certain that it was all in the bag? Of course not. But I fell asleep with a good feeling inside, in a completely positive frame of mind. For the night before a final, you couldn't really wish for more. Then, when the final itself took place the following day, it seemed to last no more than five minutes. This is what has stayed with me from those few hours that changed my life.

CHAPTER FOURTEEN

RISE LIKE A
PHOENIX

'Once I'm reborn,
You know I will rise like a phoenix'
WORDS FROM THE SONG WRITTEN BY ALEXANDER ZUCKOWSKI,
JULIAN MAAS, ROBIN GRUBERT AND CHARLIE MASON

There is a scene in David Lynch's film *Lost Highway* in which the hero is approached at a party by someone he doesn't know, who tells him something very odd: the mystery man tells him that he is at our hero's house at the same time as being at the party. To prove this, the mystery man hands him the telephone; answering the phone on the other end is the mystery man himself. I love stories where time and space cancel each other out, like a Möbius strip where you can no longer distinguish between top and bottom or between the inner and outer surfaces. It's true that we like to insist that time is linear, and every watch and every alarm clock on our planet makes that claim, but sometimes we end up in situations where things are different, where the hands do not move, where everything comes to a standstill and we find ourselves in a time bubble.

That's what happened when I stepped onto the stage on 10 May 2014. Everything seemed to have slowed right down. I seemed all of a sudden to have all the time in the world, because I was in a state that was simultaneously real and unreal. I was singing and giving it everything I had in terms of voice and emotion, and that was real. But my calmness felt as unreal as if I was in Śūnyatā, which is described in Zen teachings as 'a state of emptiness free of thoughts and temptation'. The TV recording shows that when I emerged from this time bubble, I looked nervous, jittery and out of breath, and that the precious minutes when I was performing could not be defined in terms of the usual units of time. Eventually the flames behind me and the light above me faded away, and the golden rain died down to be replaced by a storm of ecstatic public acclaim. That was the moment when the time bubble burst. I was now back in the linear normality of our reality. It was only now that the events of the evening caught up with me: someone handed me a glass of champagne – I gulped it down in one go, and immediately drank another.

René, Nicole, Tamara and Matthias stood round me and we now just had to wait while the clock hands kept ticking by at an obscenely slow pace.

Wait.

Wait.

And wait a bit more.

All at once I felt a sudden need, an urge arising from a combination of the champagne and my nerves, the latter of which had returned with a vengeance and swept away all the calm from my state of Śūnyatā.

'I have to go to the ladies!'

'Not right now!' I don't know who blurted this out, but the tone was extremely tense. 'The result could be coming at any moment.'

'I don't care. We have to run!'

The hall was so big that the technicians had to move around on small electric golf buggies. The train of my fishtail dress was three metres long and the toilets were at the farthest end of the hall; we did not just run, we sprinted. When I arrived I had to strip down completely because the dress was so tight. But I couldn't complain – after all, I had designed it myself. It had been created by the ART for ART costume studios in Vienna, which are the best in the world. The company still employs expert artisans with the traditional couture accomplishments you rarely come across in Europe these days – milliners, seamstresses and costume dyers. My design had certainly needed their expertise. The fishtail dress was made of white glitter-speckled tulle, overlaid with golden lace and covered with Swarovski crystals sewn on by hand. But now, as I began to get undressed, the microphone clip detached itself and ended up falling into... well, you can imagine where. So what did I do? I had to laugh because the situation was so wonderfully grotesque that you couldn't have made it up if you'd tried. Outside in the vestibule, I neatly cleaned and dried everything; fortunately, the sensitive electronics had not suffered any damage from coming into contact with the water. I was now well and truly relieved, in both senses of the word: if I win, I thought, I'll have to sing again, then there'll be a news conference and after that life will be like a state of emergency. There'll be no more opportunities to disappear when that happens. But at this moment in time, yes, I could go – because right now I was just one of many contestants.

A few moments later and we were back in position, the clocks ticking away as before, while the organizers whizzed up and down various European countries via their TV links. In the end, a total of thirteen countries announced: 'Twelve points go to Austria'. Even though I had visualised this earlier, even though out of all the favourites I had been regarded since the semi-final as *primus inter pares* – first among equals – and even though I had been lucky enough to have felt that magical moment of timelessness, I could still hardly believe it when the final result was announced.

Now that my victory was absolutely definite, I again felt the full force of my doubts rising up inside me: this is impossible – not you, little Tom from Styria. The one they picked on and ridiculed. The one who shocked people so much because he was different. The one who's gay. The one who's just asking for it at the railway station. The one who somehow always managed to wriggle his way out to safety, and had not just one but two coming-outs: the first to be himself as he really is, the second to reveal this mythical and magical creature, this bearded woman called Conchita who was hidden inside him. Conchita was now standing in a stunned daze right at the centre of the cheering, and had I not had René and my friends next to me, who knows what might have happened.

There was plenty going on as it was: I made a speech,

celebrated, laughed and cried – sometimes doing all four things simultaneously. Some of the words I said were recorded, others were drowned out in the chaotic pandemonium, but I most certainly did say: 'This evening belongs to those who fight for peace and justice.' Was that the sentence I had thought up in front of the mirror? No. Nothing had occurred to me when I was in front of the mirror. What I came out with was spontaneous, and once again emanated from my most deeply held convictions. I didn't realize that I was proclaiming something as honest and sincere, as inflammatory and provocative, as Martin Luther King's 'I have a dream', or Mahatma Ghandi's 'First they ignore you, then they laugh at you, then they fight you, and then you win'.

Even while the victory celebrations were still in progress, a storm of outrage was breaking out among the kind of people whose fearfulness makes them cling to the past: nationalists, xenophobes and homophobes. They were saying that the Red Army should never have left Austria – in other words, someone like me should have been nailed to the cross a long time ago, or sent to the gas chambers; should have been shot, or silenced. There was more to come: they tried to blame me for the spring flooding that affected large parts of Serbia; rightwingers claimed their bigoted attitudes were being attacked; and church fundamentalists lambasted the 'decadence of the West'. That night, my response was, 'We have no time for you now', but this soon changed to, 'We need to talk about the die-hards.' That's why, before too long, I was addressing the European Parliament and meeting UN Secretary-General Ban Ki-moon. For many people, perhaps the greatest surprise of the 2014 Eurovision Song Contest was that, from the word go, I displayed such strongly-felt political views. I strived to do more than just inspire people with my music. I want to help create a more tolerant society. There's still a long way to go, but I'm not giving up.

CHAPTER FIFTEEN

THE DAYS THAT FOLLOWED

'I saw the you in me and the me in you'

FROM THE MUSICAL *SPIDER-MAN: TURN OFF THE DARK*

Experts say we need seven to eight hours' sleep a night. From 10 May onwards, I learnt that you can also survive on far less, at least for a certain period of time. In the weeks after the contest, I would have had to create numerous copies of myself in order to meet all the interview and performance requests coming my way. These poured in from the world's largest cities and from the farthest-flung corners of the earth alike. Luckily, René decided that staying level-headed was the best approach to all the hype surrounding me. Otherwise I might have met with the same fate as the actor John Belushi, who was rushing around so much towards the end of his life that people in New York and Los Angeles could have sworn on the Bible that they had both seen him at the same time. Having success is one thing, but being able to shape your success is quite a different matter. We –

that is, my team and I – were criticised after the contest by various know-it-alls for showing no interest in making a fast buck. But we were clear in our own minds that life is less a sprint than a marathon, and it's important to pace yourself properly. Nevertheless, we still had a hectic time of it in the days after the final.

The reception in Vienna alone was mind-blowing. My adopted home city welcomed me with open arms. I attended one event after another, getting nowhere near enough sleep. First there was the annual two-day Boylesque Festival. This was followed by a talk at TEDx, an offshot of the global TED conferences, which seeks to give a platform to 'ideas worth spreading'. Then there was the annual Life Ball in Vienna which, together with the Opera Ball, forms the highlight of the city's year. The Life Ball is a combination of gala, ball, revue and party, and it's the top charity event in Europe supporting people with AIDS/HIV. It was founded by Gery Keszler and seems to get bigger each year, attracting stars such as Bill Clinton, Sharon Stone, Elton John and Catherine Deneuve. The event is held in Vienna's grand City Hall and its surrounding squares, with a magenta-coloured carpet laid out from the grand Ringstraße ring road to the main grandstand. With TV broadcasters from all around the world, countless journalists, a dense throng of celebrities, thousands and thousands of spectators, top TV ratings, and huge sums of money raised, the Life Ball is always guaranteed to dominate newspaper headlines.

As part of the event, there's also an annual fashion show, which in 2014 featured Vivienne Westwood and Jean Paul Gaultier. I'd always liked going to the Life Ball and had even appeared on stage there once, playing the lead role in a performance of *The Valiant Little Tailor*. That had been at the fairytale-themed 2007 Life Ball, whose motto was, 'Once upon a time there was a princess called Hope'. This time round, it was going to be a little different. I had been invited to sing, and so the existing programme had to be hurriedly re-arranged to incorporate my appearance. Normally everything runs like clockwork at the Life Ball but now, of all times, there were some technical hitches. When you sing live on stage, you experience the unpleasant phenomenon of not being able to hear yourself in real-time: there's always a time delay, as if you're making a phone call on a line with poor connection. At rock concerts, in order to avoid this problem, the organisers build speakers into the side of the stage that are directed at the performers rather than the audience. In sound engineering this is known as 'foldback monitoring', and if there are no speakers available you are given special earplugs that can carry out the same function. I had hardly walked out onto the stage when it became clear that the monitoring was not working. So I was now singing to a home audience of many thousands and all I could hear was cheering and shouting, applause, the accompanying music, but not myself. Every time I sang a few words I had to wait for an echo – not the best performance I've ever given. Luckily, the fans were feeling well-disposed towards me and were in full-blown party mood, because when it was all over they said: 'We didn't notice a thing, you were great!' But I was seething inside. When something like this happens, I become quiet rather than loud. My Copenhagen team – apart from Tamara who was busy elsewhere – now rallied round me and, surrounded by my friends, I quickly regained my composure.

Soon I was able to joke and laugh again and look forward to the fashion show. Naturally, considering my background, I was especially curious to see Vivienne Westwood – or, rather, Dame Commander of the Order of the British Empire Vivienne Westwood. Possibly because, just like me, she rose from very humble beginnings. Her mother Dora was a weaver, a notoriously tough profession, while her father Gordon came from a family of shoemakers: hardly an illustrious background. In any case, Vivienne's progress to the top of the fashion world was not easy. As a young mother of two, she decided to make clothes for her children. At some point, she began taking traditional designs and combining them with unusual fabrics and her own original ideas for patterns and shapes. This was what led to her big breakthrough. Despite her phenomenal success, she lived for more than thirty years in a simple council flat. All of this was running through the back of my mind as she took me to one side after the fashion show.

'You're the star they're all talking about', she said, eyeing me from head to toe. 'I'd like to give you some good advice.' You get to hear a lot of good advice over the course of your life, and it isn't always welcome. Yet I'd taken to Vivienne immediately. She reminded me of my grandma and, just like her, she smelled of that wonderful mixture of menthol and eau de cologne – a hallmark of people of her generation. I answered respectfully that I would be very glad to hear her advice.

'Embrace everything while you can. It can all disappear quicker than you think.'

'That's exactly what I intend to do.' My answer was heartfelt. Someone like Vivienne knows what she's talking about. After all, it was way back in 1973 that she'd named her boutique Too Fast To Live, Too Young To Die, in reference to James Dean, who's life was cut short aged twenty-four. The stardust of today is the dust that lines the streets tomorrow. She and I got on like a house on fire and could have talked all day and night, despite all the hectic activity that is part and parcel of such events. She told me about her latest creation, a nineenth century tea set made of extremely thin eggshell porcelain. At this point, a horde of photographers came rushing towards us, with one of them wanting to know what the chain around her neck was supposed to signify.

'Well, what will this be meant to be?' she answered mischievously, leaving the question open. Any answer she'd given would have got lost in the meaninglessness of its interpretation. I liked her English sense of humour, and when she asked if I'd like to accompany her to a fashion show in Milan, I said yes immediately. After all, it was she who'd advised me to embrace everything while I could.

There was something else I took away from that night, something of extraordinary value: the friendship of a remarkable man – Jean Paul Gaultier. Jean Paul and I already look back on a history together, but it's only recently that we really came to know each other. I had of course always been a fan of his. He on the other hand had only watched my first attempt to participate in the Eurovision Song Contest and invited me to Paris after that. Back then we hadn't had time for intense and meaningful discussions, which is what we wanted to make amends for now. It didn't take long to discover that we had a lot in common.

After the fashion show we found a bit of time to talk, again to find a lot of common ground. 'The funny thing', said Jean Paul, 'is that I don't have any training as a fashion designer. I always liked sketching, and found the human body interesting. So I started off doing shaded drawings of bodies, and afterwards added clothing to them. Then I sent off my sketches to a few people to look at.'

Jean Paul is a perfect example of talent and hard work combining in perfect harmony. Pierre Cardin, the fashion designer who launched the first haute couture enterprise selling prêt-à-porter garments to the masses, hired him as an assistant, and the rest is history: in 1976 Jean Paul presented his own collection, and today he is now one of the few people in fashion to personally run a worldwide operation. His company recently announced it wants to give up its prêt-à-porter division in order to concentrate exclusively on haute couture. It'll be interesting to see how this works out, particularly for me: a few months after our first meeting, I appeared at Le Crazy Horse cabaret in Paris wearing one of Jean Paul's custom-made designer dresses. This wasn't something we discussed during that first conversation, having only just met. Nevertheless, we could sense that we liked each other and would like to work together at some point in the future. A spark of friendship had already been ignited during our arrival at the Life Ball.

The organizers had timed things in such a way that, even though our arrival would not be simultaneous, we would step onto the carpet at the same time. This was a tricky task which resulted in a bit of confusion. Straight after the parade, the magenta-coloured carpet had to be replaced by a blue one. While Jean Paul and I were walking through the crowd of onlookers, the Berlin photographer Julian Laidig, a close friend of mine, was standing close by. Very shortly afterwards, he was to take the best photo I've ever seen, one that could only have been taken by someone with a trained eye and a perfect sense of timing. Julian says that 'photography is more than just pressing a button', and this picture is the proof. It captures the precise point at which another one of those miraculous time bubbles was formed. I was right in the middle of the bubble when the chaos erupted. The onlookers were pushing from behind, while Gery Keszler wanted me both to stay put and to carry on walking and was unable to decide between the two. René was just the opposite: he shouted out an instruction to me which I could not hear, and in the end I just detached from the situation completely. Behind me, Jean Paul was holding onto the train of my dress, while Matthias was tugging at it from the front. This moment was, of course, just another fleeting instant in my life, but Julian managed to capture it for ever and, what's more, to use this moment to convey a sense of eternity. Previously, I had only experienced this time bubble from the inside; being able to observe it from the outside is a rare stroke of luck. Jean Paul liked the photo too, and when the opportunity presented itself, I gave him a really huge print of it.

It's rare to meet people like Jean Paul, people with whom you can have such a genuinely good time. When the opportunity later arose to spend a night out on the town with him in Vienna, I grabbed it with both hands. But that was still a while off, and right now I had just one thing on my mind: to finally catch up on some proper sleep.

CHAPTER SIXTEEN

PARIS, OOH-LA-LA

'There's no business like show business'

FROM THE MUSICAL ANNIE GET YOUR GUN

From our very first meeting at the Life Ball, it was clear that Jean Paul and I were going to be friends. Soon afterwards, he invited me to appear in his haute couture fashion show. Just like all the other models, I was given a comp card displaying my body measurements and shoe size. While I'm obviously no stranger to the world of fashion, I was unbelievably excited. Models who work for big designer brands are professionals, whereas I was almost a complete novice on the catwalk. The very fact that we westerners are used to starting out on our heels before transferring our weight to the balls of our feet makes the way we walk look a bit ungraceful. In Asia they often do things differently – you start off gently on the balls of your feet before bringing your heels down. While this can feel a little strange to us, it's better for the back and allows models to virtually float down the catwalk. Yet this approach also contains an element of danger, as I was about to discover.

Jean Paul is one of the few designers to put on shows in his own premises, in the tradition of early Chanel fashion house shows. On the ground floor are the makeup and changing rooms, which can get as busy as a tube station at rush hour. The hall where the fashion show is held is one floor higher. The guests were already in their seats and the models were being asked to line up in the stairway. Because I was in such a lavish dress, an anxious-looking stage manager led me past all the models and parked me in a wall recess.

He just had time to say, 'I'll call you on', before he disappeared. Shortly afterwards, the first model walked onto the catwalk; a few seconds later I heard the stage manager shout out: 'Oh my God, she's fallen!' I felt myself go weak at the knees: firstly, because my thoughts went out to the poor model and, secondly, because I realised that if a professional can fall over, the same could easily happen to me. I then heard a second cry: 'She's fallen again.' I was now getting really panicky. Yet there was no way I could make a run for it without attracting attention. The models were moving past me like beads on a string, while those who had already done their bit on the catwalk rushed down the stairs as if bitten by a snake, hurrying off to climb into their next outfit.

To anyone who thinks modelling is an easy career – I'm afraid I have to disappoint you. I've now seen for myself how difficult it is. In those moments of extreme pressure, no thought is given to anything or anybody. If one of the girls fractures a toe while running, she'll just grin and bear it and walk smiling down the catwalk a few minutes later as if nothing had happened. When it comes to their work, these girls are tough, and I liked that. A short time afterwards, we heard news that there had been a third fall. This time round, I no longer contemplated doing a runner, but thought only of doing what I had to do, and doing it well. It later transpired that the reflective foil used to cover the catwalk had not been stretched tightly enough in one place, causing any model unfortunate enough to dig her heel into that precise spot to stumble. Luckily for me, I stepped over it, managing to walk successfully down the catwalk as the final model of the show. Jean Paul ran up behind me and grabbed hold of the train of my dress – it was a dream of a wedding dress, black, gold and crimson, draped with lots of lace and sharply tapered hems, and complete with – my favourite part – a veil. He then went ahead and actually knelt down before me. On receiving this honour, I became a little flustered. The way I see it, I've only just started doing my bit to make the world a more beautiful place, whereas Jean Paul has been doing this for decades. Despite this, he still retains an utterly infectious enthusiasm, the sort only possessed by those who are doing exactly what they were destined to do.

The effort that goes into achieving such magical moments never ceases to fascinate me. People in the audience are not allowed to either see or feel this: everything must appear to run of its own accord. In actual fact, a team of highly qualified specialists is working behind the scenes to inject some magic into our reality. I was now gradually getting to know more and more of these people, and one of the very first I became acquainted with was Camille Gilbert, whom I met at Jean Paul's fashion show. She was responsible for my hair, a wig that Jean Paul had selected himself. As Camille painstakingly arranged every last strand, I couldn't resist asking her one question: 'Do you know that your beautiful name comes from the attendants guarding the temples in ancient Rome?'

The French always seem somewhat surprised when someone speaks their language. My knowledge of French at the time was still 'un peu rouillé' – a little bit rusty – but this soon changed as I began to visit their country more frequently. I like chatting to the people who go to such lengths to take care of me, and this was also the case with Anny Errandonea, whom I met a few weeks later at Karl Lagerfeld's. Her sole responsibility was to attend to my fingernails. She reminded me of a French headmistress – or at least how I imagined a French headmistress to be – addressing me haughtily in a harsh Parisian dialect without seeming too bothered about whether I understood her or not. She asked me to show her my hand, so I held it out to her. Raising one critical eyebrow, she stared at it intensely for what appeared to be a short eternity… and then let it drop back down.

'C'est parfait', she hissed, everything is in perfect order – but that's not how it sounded to me. I was startled. Was she annoyed because I looked after my hands and was putting her out of a job? There's a popular French saying – 'C'est le ton qui fait la chanson' – that translates roughly as, 'It's not what you say, but how you say it'. Right now, her voice didn't sound particularly friendly. However, this soon changed once I started up a conversation with her. After some initial hesitancy, she came out of herself more and more, and I was yet again able to note how much people are willing to open up if you show some interest in them. Sifting gracefully through a potpourri of clothes, wigs, accessories, makeup paraphernalia and all the other things you might need for a fashion shoot, she soon started telling me about her life, where she'd started out, and what she thought of people who did not take care of themselves: *'Absolument rien'*. Nothing at all.

I had to smile as I'd obviously misunderstood her *'C'est parfait'* reaction. She now became less and less inhibited, and started to pay me compliments about my skin, eyelashes, hair – even my teeth. In the presence of an elegant woman, my thoughts returned automatically to my grandma, who also attached importance to a neat appearance. 'It's a mark of respect to others,' is what she'd say, and I like this way of thinking. If you go round looking sloppy, you're acting sloppily towards those around you, which isn't right. At the end of our session, Anny wished me a warm goodbye, French style: a peck on the right, left, right and then left again, just as they do in Paris. In case anyone is planning on going to Provence, there it's two kisses, starting with the left cheek. In Brest and Poitou it's just one kiss, but in the Massif Central, Arles and the Drôme, Hérault, Gard, Vaucluse and Hautes-Alpes, it's three. I was glad of this opportunity to study the customs of the French, because very soon I would be going down south. The blue waters of the Mediterranean Sea – *La Grande Bleue,* as they say poetically in France – were beckoning.

CHAPTER SEVENTEEN

OFF TO CANNES!

'And whatever I've got to do,
I've got a lovely day to do it in, that's true'

FROM THE MUSICAL *CALL ME MADAM*

Cannes, the pearl of the Côte d'Azur: when it's the annual International Film Festival, everyone wants to go; when it's the Cannes Lions International Advertising Festival, everyone wants to go; when it's the world's biggest music fair – Midem, *le Marché international de l'édition musicale* – then, of course, everyone wants to go. Luckily, when the 2014 amfAR Cinema Against AIDS gala was held, everyone wanted to go to Cannes as well.

The organisation amfAR is the world's leading nonprofit organization dedicated to the support of HIV/AIDS research. The amount of work still to be done in this area is revealed by some staggering statistics. There are currently 35 million people living with HIV world-wide, of whom one-tenth are younger than 15. Each year, more than 2 million people will become infected, with 1.5 million deaths. Just one-third of all those infected have access to antiretroviral therapy. This isn't a problem that's confined to far-off countries: it's also happening right on our doorstep. The number of HIV-infected people, both hetero- and homosexual, is on the rise in Western Europe. So, when all those prominent people line up to attend the amfAR gala, what's it all about? It's quite simple: AIDS research costs a lot of money, and this gala raises a lot of money.

When Life Ball founder Gery Keszler invited me to attend, I agreed straight away. One of the first people I bumped into was American actress Rosario Dawson. She's appeared in films such as *Men in Black*, *Sin City*, *Percy Jackson* and *Alexander*, but what I particularly like is her serious commitment to a considerable number of charitable organizations, such as Oxfam and Amnesty International. Rosario is a good example of how you can give something back if you have made it to the top. Still, to pave the way for a redistribution of resources, to support the poor and the sick, to refuse to look the other way – does this really require being in fabulous surroundings in one of the most beautiful regions of the world? Since this is all still new to me, I'm allowed to ask myself such questions. The setting for the gala was the Hôtel du Cap-Eden-Roc, which is in Cap d'Antibes, east of Cannes. It was truly beautiful. At first I had no idea where to look: the car park itself was a feast for the eye, never mind the 140-year-old hotel. Luckily, Gery was at my side and immediately took me under his wing. Even though we were dressed up to the nines, we set out across the park, climbing over rocks and running across fields until, all of a sudden, we were standing on a steep cliff overlooking the sea. Now at least it was clear why they call it *La Grande Bleue*: as far as the eye could see, water sparkled in the glistening sunshine, flecked with snowy-white.

'Those are the yachts of the guests', said Gery. 'Come on! We don't want to miss anyone.'

It was a Who's Who of world stars. On one side, there was the former French president's wife Carla Bruni-Sarkozy, standing next to John Travolta. On the other, there was a small gathering that included Sharon Stone, Justin Bieber, Catherine Deneuve, Kylie Minogue, Bar Refaeli, Chris Tucker and Dita Von Teese. If I couldn't recognise a face, Gery would help me out.

'That's Harvey Weinstein', he muttered. 'One of Hollywood's most influential film producers. *Pulp Fiction, The English Patient, Gangs of New York, Sin City* and *Django Unchained*.' He then pointed to an elegant figure dressed all in silver:

'And that is …'

'Carine Roitfeld', I said. Perhaps I even gave a brief, not particularly ladylike whistle through my teeth. For ten years, Carine had been editor-in-chief of *Vogue Paris*, the world's most important fashion magazine. Here at the Ball she was running a fashion show called 'The Red Collection', a compilation of the finest designer items from the top fashion labels, all in bright red. They were auctioned off at the end of the evening and raised $5 million for the charity. English artist Damien Hirst's gilded skeleton of a mammoth brought in another $11 million. At the close of the event, the proud organizers made an emotional announcement: 'A new record! We've raised a total of $35 million.'

This figure provided the answer to whether events like this should be held in such magnificent surroundings: yes, definitely. It attracts the people you need to make things happen big time. The $35 million that were raised are equivalent to keeping alive the hope that a little more progress might be made in HIV research. I let myself be carried along by the throng of people, surprised and touched that I was being allowed to take part. Then something started to happen that at first I couldn't quite believe: stars I knew from the cinema, from television, from the stage, were asking if they could possibly have their photo taken with me. The first few times I replied: 'You're asking me? I'm the one who should be asking you!' After that, I restricted myself to 'Of course!' Suddenly, the lady in silver was in front of me asking the same question. This time I replied: '*Enchantée, Madame Roitfeld, heureuse de vous connaître*, only too glad to take a photo.'

And that was how we got chatting. Over the course of our conversation, I noticed Carine surveying me with attentive glances. During her years working at Vogue, she had created a type of woman with a totally new look, a style she called erotic-porno-chic: sexy, elegant, lots of eyeliner, a diva who knows what she wants and what she's capable of. A strong woman, which was exactly what Carine herself proved herself to be very shortly afterwards. A stranger in a dinner jacket joined us. Gery had disappeared into the crowd of people, so I never got to find out who this person was. The stranger passed on greetings to me from Karl Lagerfeld, who regretted he could not be here, but who, he said, would like to work with me at some later stage. At this point, Carine interrupted the man's flow of words.

'Would you like meet Karl?' she asked me, and, without waiting for a reply, she linked her arm through mine: '*I'm* your new best friend and *I'm* the one who'll introduce you to him.'

We now made an abrupt about turn, something Carine was able to accomplish despite her incredibly tall high heels – her golden rule is ten centimetres during the day, and higher in the evening. For that matter, the heels I was wearing weren't exactly short, either. We left the man in the dinner jacket standing there. After all, it's a known fact that whenever someone claims they will introduce X to Y, nothing ever happens. Carine Roitfeld is different. She's a woman who gets things done. Two days later, I got a phone call to fix a date with her and Karl Lagerfeld. I was overwhelmed! Karl Lagerfeld provides the two letters that mean everything in the world of fashion – KL. No more is necessary.

CHAPTER EIGHTEEN

KL & CR

'Ring out the old, bring in the new'
FROM THE MUSICAL *SUNSET BOULEVARD*

'I'm no generation's child,' Karl Lagerfeld once said. 'I belong nowhere and can fit in anywhere.'

What a relaxed attitude from a man who, despite having achieved everything, still buzzes with ideas from one day to the next. He was and still is a fashion designer for Pierre Balmain, Jean Patou, Chloé, Fendi, Chanel and, of course, his own label. He works as a costumier for theatre and opera. He's a perfumer, designer, bookseller, publisher, photographer: a universal genius who says of himself, 'I've always drawn despite never having had an art teacher. I was born with a pencil in my hand. I learned it all by myself.'

There are clearly more of these people out there than we think: people who teach themselves and are forever motivated. People who were often – perhaps for that very reason – teased at school. Karl was branded the *Glückskuh*

– the 'lucky cow' – as his father owned the Glücksklee condensed-milk factory (*Glücksklee* is the German word for four-leaf clover). Frequently, such people go their own way in life and refuse to be confined to a single box. Karl is another person in my life who's partial to traditional fragrances in his nostrils, with menthol and eau de cologne, as well as with Lanvin Arpège, a perfume created in 1927, which his mother wore and with which she even sprinkled the curtains in her home. 'The whole house smelled wonderful,' he recalled, and, of course, it reminded me of my grandmother and I immediately felt at ease in his presence.

Anyone visiting his premises in Paris for the first time would certainly be surprised to see so many books on view. There might be 300,000 of them, estimates Karl, who told me that, by the age of six, he'd already read classics of German literature such as *Die Buddenbrooks* by Thomas Mann and *Die Nibelungen* with illustrations by Moritz von Schwind and Schnorr von Carolsfeld. He was thrilled to meet me: 'Now we can talk German together, that's fantastic!' Everything had already been set up, and Carine gave me a final debrief. For her magazine, *CR Fashion Book*, I was to pose in front of the camera with the New Zealand model Ashleigh Good. The face of Prada and Chanel, Ashleigh has frequently worked with Karl. Yet this was something new even for her: a photo session while five months pregnant.

'We'll call the photos,' said Carine, with a slight smile on her face, '"The New Normal."' It's a name you could only come up with if you're someone who thinks in unconventional terms, as there was nothing at all 'normal' about these photos – partly because I presented a Conchita I had actually intended to keep to myself: without makeup, vulnerable, yet strong. Little Tom from Bad Mitterndorf, now matured into a grown man, with beard, long hair and well-defined muscles. I wouldn't have done that shoot with anyone except Karl Lagerfeld, someone in whom I had complete trust. One of the shots called for me to pose on Ashleigh's lap – I was so, so cautious. What a wonderful radiance shines from a pregnant woman! No, in the end there was nothing 'normal' about those photos: exceptional and brave, they suit both me and Ashleigh. A year before, she'd appeared alongside Kati Nescher in the spring 2013 Chanel haute couture collection as a lesbian bride. That's also one of the purposes of the fashion industry: to show us that there's more out there than just standardised lifestyles, which so often don't work.

For me, it was a pleasure working with Karl. He's a workaholic, and anyone with as many projects on the go as he has can't afford to waste time. His assistants – including Anny Errandonea, with whom I was now getting along like a house on fire – know which things are important. In the studio, Karim was in control of everything: he did the lighting, he focused the camera, while Karl shot one photo after another. Going about his work with total confidence, he told me: 'You need to know what you can do, otherwise you're better off leaving it alone.' Sounds simple, but it's more difficult to put into practice than you think. It's a mindset that probably only bears fruit once you've got Karl's experience and can think as quickly as him, while still being fun to be with and never losing touch, always keeping your feet on the ground. He's a true role model! While he shot the photos, Carine made sure the outfits were in the right place at the right time. She had everything under control and would keep calling out for more: 'The Rick Owens skirt,' she shouted, 'with the Givenchy veil!' During a break, she told me about her plans for the CR *Fashion Book* and her passion for Céline Dion. 'By the age of 20, she'd already brought out 14 albums, won 15 Félix music awards, and had three platinum and four gold discs under her belt. Despite that, she was unknown in the USA – because she sang in French.'

We talked about English being the world language, and I told her that, after 'Rise Like a Phoenix', my next song would also be in English.

'Go for it,' she encouraged me. 'It's the right decision.'

I went on to tell her how I had once followed in Céline's footsteps. 'It was a moment that steered my life in a new direction,' I began. I was on my way to *Die Große Chance*, the talent show on Austrian TV. After spending hours on my makeup, I had taken one last look in the mirror before leaving the house. I was happy with the way I looked, even though, by my current standards, I wasn't made up at all. Arriving in front of the TV studios, I found a few hundred people waiting out there. All of them talented, all of them ready to give their best. I hesitated a moment before joining the queue.

'That moment,' Carine chipped in, 'was your point of no return, right?'

The throng of fellow hopefuls was daunting, and there were some who actually gave up and went home. Yes, joining that queue had been my personal point of no return. 'For Céline, it was the moment she brought out her first album in English,' said Carine. 'It went platinum in the USA, and the single 'Where Does My Heart Beat Now' jumped to number 4. And yet she remained true to herself.' That's what I especially like about her international career. 'The same year, she was set to receive the Félix Award for best anglophone artist, but she turned it down, saying that she was a francophone singer and always would be. *Elle est courageuse.* She's very brave. Very true to herself. What was it like as you followed in her footsteps?'

'To begin with, it meant waiting,' I said, returning to my story. 'Waiting, waiting, waiting, as usual where TV is concerned. Then it was finally my turn to perform in front of the preliminary judges. They asked me to perform a song so they could make a decision. If they gave it the thumbs down, that would mean the end for me. If they liked it, I was still in with a chance of singing in front of the real judges.' So I sang 'And I Am Telling You I'm Not Going' from the musical *Dreamgirls*, about a 1960s girl group, The Dreamettes, taking part in a talent show. It's based on the true story of the Supremes and the incomparable Diana Ross. The idea of singing a song about a talent show at a talent show appealed to me, and it obviously also went down well with the preliminary judges. I was still in the race.

'Then there was another long wait, but finally it was my turn. This time I sang Céline's 'My Heart Will Go On', perhaps her greatest hit. The song was written for the James Cameron movie *Titanic*, and apparently Céline didn't even want to be the one to sing it at first – which just goes to show that everyone has their points of no return in life. She changed her mind, the film became one of the biggest cinema hits of all time and the song itself won both a Grammy and an Oscar.

What more could you ask for? Anyway, the day I sang it, the same song gave my career a helping hand, because the judges were won over, giving me a standing ovation, something you don't get every day from people in that position. That put me in the final, which, of course, meant a lot more hanging around. I remember spending the evening with friends over a drink in Café Blaustern, somewhat stunned by how far I'd got.'

'Back then, had you already thought about where Conchita might go from there?' asked Carine.

'To be honest, no,' I replied. 'Sometimes I still can't quite believe it.'

Although Carine's not the 'let me take you in my arms' type, that's just what she now did – before immediately bellowing out yet more instructions to her assistants: 'Get me the Walter Steiger shoes! The Chantal Thomass stockings! The Prada dress! The Scott Stevenson bodysuit!'

We carried on working. Have I mentioned how strenuous it is to be a model? As the day drew to a close, I was just as tired as after the talent show. Yet there was one big difference: it felt much more like I was being me.

CHAPTER NINETEEN

MY LIFE AS A NOMAD

'Who can explain it,
Who can tell you why,
Fools give you reasons,
Wise men never try.'
FROM THE MUSICAL *SOUTH PACIFIC*

Max Schruff was the name of my English teacher at school in Bad Mitterndorf. Anyone with a name like that has got be a little bit strict. And so he was. Every Friday he'd give us a vocabulary test, and if we'd been asleep at our desks from Monday to Thursday, we were in trouble. Perhaps the reason why my teacher was so into discipline was that he'd had to fight his way back after a sporting accident. People who do that are always keen to pass on their experiences. Max Schruff taught me a lot and I'm still grateful to him, because, without English, I wouldn't be where I am now. For me, the question of whether or not we make Europe a success depends on our ability to communicate with each other across national borders. Ultimately, prejudice stems from a failure to talk and to understand.

When I recently appeared in front of the European Parliament, I was again made aware of this peculiar fact about Europe: the Parliament has twenty-four official languages. In order of year of national accession, they are: German, French, Italian, Dutch, Danish, English, Greek, Portuguese, Spanish, Finnish, Swedish, Estonian, Latvian, Lithuanian, Maltese, Polish, Slovak, Slovenian, Czech, Hungarian, Bulgarian, Irish, Romanian and Croatian. Under the European constitution, all documents must be translated into all official languages – a huge task. But it's the only way to make sure that MEPs and staff are able to follow the Parliament's work and read all the documents.

Yet when it comes to speaking, it's usually English that takes over. The reason is obvious: English is the international language of our age. I once learned that it's the world's most frequently spoken language and that over eighty per cent of electronically stored information is in English. In short, we'd be lost without English – which reminds me of Max Schruff. There are unlikely to be many pupils – and I was no exception – who think they'll one day get to chat to the UN Secretary-General or appear on a UK talk show. And it's equally unlikely that many teachers would get very far by trying to make their pupils believe that that's exactly what will one day happen to them, saying: 'It's life you're learning for, not school'. So there must be another approach, like the one Max Schruff used.

These thoughts went through my mind when the BBC invited me on *The One Show*. Chatting spontaneously with national celebrities on live TV in a foreign language is an art in itself. I did well enough to make presenter Alex Jones forget that I came from faraway Austria. I couldn't help but smile, witnessing once again how useful those much-hated Friday vocabulary tests really were. That same day, I'd already been interviewed by a host of radio stations, TV channels and newspapers when, all of a sudden, there she was sitting next to me: Sophie Ellis-Bextor. She was also a guest on *The One Show*. If I'd been a little drowsy beforehand, I was now once again wide awake. I used to listen to Sophie Ellis-Bextor as a teenager in the Green Cave while working on new designs. She's a wonderful songwriter. I remember how excited I was when her last album came out. Called *Wanderlust*, it used one of the few German words that have made it into the English language (alongside *autobahn* and *bratwurst*).

Perhaps I should have seized the opportunity to invite Sophie to Bad Mitterndorf, where I could have been her hiking guide in an Alpine remake of *Wild Girls*. Sadly, it wasn't to be, as I was yet again asked to explain what had happened on the day of the Eurovision Song Contest. This was still a question that put me on the spot. Had that evening turned my life upside down? Or was it just a normal progression in my career?

They say that memory often lies, and we're made aware of this whenever we speak about past events. Depending on my mood on the day, I sometimes still feel stunned and say: 'But I've never won anything.' Or I might simply think of it as something I just stumbled into. These thoughts were whizzing around my head when I appeared as a guest on the *The Graham Norton Show* a few days later. Graham is an

Irish comedian, and I'm a big fan of his. He also commentates on the Eurovision Song Contest for the BBC, so he's familiar with it, which spared me some of the usual questions. On top of that, he's just a fun person to be around.

British comedians always take things just that little bit further than in other countries, and I like that. In the 1970s, Graham Chapman, John Cleese, Terry Gilliam, Eric Idle, Terry Jones and Michael Palin from Monty Python began playing women on TV in the UK – something that even today is unthinkable in some countries. The Pythons called these female roles 'pepperpots', and I'm sure they'd think of me one as one of those pepperpot ladies: fiery and sharp-tongued. Yet on the evening in question, after taking her seat next to the other guest on the show, the actress Kirsten Dunst, my pepperpot lady was suddenly very quiet and reserved. I'd seen Kirsten in Lars von Trier's film *Melancholia*, in *Spider-Man 3* and in *Bachelorette*, and I greatly admired her versatility. I just wish I could have told her so, but I found her accent almost incomprehensible. So there we were, a cosy threesome, having being joined by the comedienne Dawn French. There were plenty of laughs, but I didn't get to exchange a single word with Kirsten. Matthias and Tamara pulled me up about it after the show.

'I'd have loved to chat with her,' I told them. 'But I just couldn't!'

Matthias smiled: 'She's got German roots, you know. Even German citizenship.'

'Okay, I'll try it in my Styrian dialect next time. Or perhaps I need more help from Max Schruff,' having told my friends about my English teacher.

'Did he teach you Spanish as well?' enquired Tamara.

'No, why?'

'Because you're now off to Spain. Followed by Italy, Finland and Belgium.'

I enjoyed my nomadic lifestyle, even though it took its toll on me. There was a string of unforgettable surprises, like the one I'd had a few hours before, when, on going into my dressing room, I'd found a bunch of orchids together with a card saying, 'Congratulations, we love you, Elton & David.' Here was another thing I'd never dared dream of at school: that Sir Elton John and his partner David Furnish would one day devote a few lines to me. While many people may idolise Elton John for having sold more records than most other pop artists, now supposedly in excess of 900 million, I respect him because he's a brilliant musician and an outstanding singer, because people listen to what he has to say and because he knows how to channel his influence towards important things, such as the Elton John AIDS Foundation, which has so far collected over 275 million dollars and supports projects in more than fifty countries around the world. It's clear to me that someone like that must be a very busy person, which made it even more special to receive his attention. Not forgetting the orchids! I adore the 'queen of flowers' and what it represents: the love and beauty of young women in Chinese garden art – and ὄρχις, i.e. testicles, in the late Greek classical period. 'It doesn't come much better than this,' I told myself. 'This is the ideal flower for Conchita Wurst!'

The next days and weeks saw me continue my travels, to Spain, Italy and Finland, followed by Belgium, Sweden and

France. I behaved like the perfect European, going from country to country, full of curiosity and without prejudice. While bringing my own culture with me, I also respected that of my host country. And despite rejoicing at the ease with which I was able to travel, I never forgot how fragile this European construct of ours is. Whenever the talk turns to 'closing borders' and 'imposing travel restrictions', this usually reflects a fear that someone undesirable might come along. But whereas fear is a poor adviser, joy is just the opposite.

The longer I toured Europe, the clearer it became to me how important our togetherness is. If we put our disagreements aside for a moment, we actually have a lot in common. Wherever I went, I came across people with ideas, inspiring views and a desire to create something – like at the Bjorn Borg Fashion Show in Stockholm. Bjorn was one of the best tennis players in the world. He played in the Davis Cup at just fifteen years of age before going on to win Wimbledon five times in a row from 1976 to 1980. He notched up eleven Grand Slam titles and sixty-four singles tournament victories. But what impressed me even more was that, compared with other tennis pros, he decided to cut his sporting career short, retiring at just twenty-six years of age so he could turn his attention to other things, such as fashion. Today, the whole world pays attention when the Bjorn Borg Fashion Show opens its doors. It was my pleasure to be a front row guest of honour at the show. 'Conchita, Gaultier, Lagerfeld, Borg, where will this end?' posted a fan on my Facebook page. Although this meant 'which show will you be at next', the question was also open to a different interpretation: when are you going to give yourself a break? Isn't it getting too much for you? My answer was, quite honestly, 'No!' Of course, I sometimes got tired – I'm not a machine. But I found the work fun, and someone who's having fun also has energy. That's one of the laws of life.

When I was invited to the Fête de la Musique in Montpellier, one of the biggest series of concerts in France, Nicole took a photo of me in the hotel room looking pretty exhausted.

That's quite plausible, because I'd just been performing on stage in the city centre. It was my first time visiting Montpellier, which is located in southern France, and I immediately fell in love with the place. It has a magnificent medieval city centre, with splendid buildings around the Place de la Comédie. Next door to it, in an almost seamless transition, is the Antigone district, a modern version of ancient Greece. With the sea just around the corner, the temperature is agreeable even in winter, and there's always music in the air – especially during the Fête de la Musique, which that year featured wonderful musicians such as François Valéry, Yannick Noah, Alizée and Chico & The Gypsies.

Despite attending the festival to perform, politics also played a role during my visit, as is so often the case in France. During an interview that I gave the newspaper *Le Monde*, the reporters came back to their favourite topic. When I'd said, 'We are unstoppable', had my words been directed at Vladimir Putin, President of the Russian Federation?

'Of course,' I replied, 'but at many other people as well.' Defamatory articles had been written about me, I'd received death threats, and so I responded to the reporter: 'If I'm their biggest problem, they've got every reason to be happy, haven't they?' When you consider the many genuine problems facing Europe and the world? Actually, I continued, I should feel honoured by the attacks against me. These people obviously think a drag queen is powerful enough to change people's attitudes across entire countries. What an honour! I added that, 'in reality, it takes more than an appearance on Eurovision, it even takes more than Eurovision itself, to bring about change.'

After all, the Song Contest had very soon been followed by European elections in which extreme rightwing and anti-European parties had won a lot of support. To avoid giving a wrong impression, I'd like to say this: I don't go around wagging my finger at people, that's really not what I want to do. What's important to me is my music, with which I set out to entertain and give pleasure. Nonetheless, as a bearded female, I'm constantly attempting to be at the forefront of social change, and the questions I get from journalists and the invitations I receive to political centres of power are proof enough of this. It therefore seems fitting that the life of a drag queen is one of constant pain. It hurts turning Tom Neuwirth into Conchita Wurst: the tight-fitting wig; the makeup, which attacks my skin; the heavy eyelashes, the bodice, the high heels. Does a drag queen need to have a certain tendency towards self-flagellation? Perhaps. It's torture, even if it doesn't look like it.

That evening in Montpellier, as I flopped down on my hotel bed after giving my show and interviews, it wasn't the day itself that had tired me out, but that stunning Jean Paul Gaultier dress, which, several hours earlier, had set Nicole cursing: it was much too tight even for me, someone who can usually easily fit into anything. Struggling with hooks and eyelets, Nicole had told me to hold my breath for minutes on end. When I finally took off the dress, there were streaks of blood where the fastener had been.

'Just like Sisi,' said Nicole, and I nodded wearily.

Sisi, Empress Elisabeth of Austria, whose image has been shaped by the films with Romy Schneider to such an extent that you almost forget her obsession with youth, her eating disorders and the girdles she used to put on to make herself fit into even the tightest of dresses.

'If Jean Paul ever comes to visit me in Vienna,' I groaned, 'I'll take him to the Sisi Museum. That really is a must-see for him.' Not that I thought such a visit was imminent. And then, suddenly, it happened.

Top: For the ARTE programme *Durch die Nacht mit* I spent a night on the town with Jean Paul Gaultier. The evening ended like every evening in Vienna should end: at a sausage stand, with beer, cheese kransky, brown bread, hot mustard and sour gherkins (or *Saure Gurkerl*, as we say). Just in case you're planning something similar yourself.

Below: That the life of a drag queen is a life of pain is demonstrated by this photo, taken after my appearance at La Fête de la Musique in Montpellier. The wig, the makeup, the eyelashes, the bodice, the high heels... they all start to hurt after a while. Even this marvellous Jean Paul Gaultier dress. On taking it off, I found streaks of blood where the fastener had been.

Top left: Jean Paul Gaultier and I got to know each other at the Vienna Life Ball, where my friend Julian Laidig shot that terrific photo. Here's me presenting a copy of it to Jean Paul. In XXXXXL format – when you're giving something to a friend, it's the only way.

Top right: Back to Amsterdam! The Boat Pride got the entire city on its feet, dressed in rainbow colours and in the best of spirits. While other parades make their way through cities in cars and trucks, in Amsterdam the floats make their way through the canals on boats. It's such fun! Especially for Nicole and for Benny, who runs my office at home in Vienna. At the closing event, after performing alongside Anastacia, Boy George and Ian McKellen, I asked: 'Will the day dawn when we no longer need parades? Will the day dawn when homosexuality is simply normal?'

Below: Even though the photo suggests otherwise, when I returned for the reception in my hometown of Bad Mitterndorf it was one of the most challenging days of my life. Everyone was out in the streets and the organisers did a fantastic job. I went on stage with my cousins, sang with the choir and was awarded an honorary citizenship. Still, it wasn't easy even during these hours of happiness to forget the difficult days of my youth.

Above: 'I want you all to shout so loud I can still hear you when I'm putting the photo on my wall!' At every concert I ask the audience to turn up the volume. The Danube Island Festival in Vienna was no exception. And they really did give it all they had – I can still hear them now!

Middle left: Pride Season is over! Manchester was the last stop on my pride tour through Europe. At the press conference, I once again made it clear that Conchita Wurst is a resolute opponent of violence and discrimination. She stands for love and acceptance.

Below left and right: Backstage during a couple of photo shoots. I'm obviously a smartphone addict, something I hadn't realised until then (insert smiley). Every photo shoot involves a lot of time spent just hanging around, so I use the opportunity to keep in touch with my fans.

Top: The mayor of Vienna Michael Haupl invited me into the Red Salon in the city hall to give me an award for my commitment to 'respect and coexistence'. As well as thanking me for this, he also asked me to continue to stand up to any negative reactions I received: 'Thank you for showing the courage to endure,' he said in his speech.

Centre and below: Ulrike Lunacek is Vice-President of the European Parliament. Together with MEPs from four of the represented parties, she invited me to Parliament. There was a huge crowd of people there and I sang and then gave a speech. My message to the parliamentarians was this: I am calling for greater commitment to the rights of homosexuals. 'It's your job,' I said, 'to fight for a functioning democracy and equal rights.'

Below: For my social media fans I have set up the series 'Conchita Wurst answers'. There are answers here to all sorts of questions. One of my favourites is: 'Have you ever fallen asleep with make-up on?' And the answer is… well, best if you go online and check it out for yourself!

Above: The photographer Pierre Commoy and the painter Gilles Blanchard build the sets at the Crazy Horse revue theatre in Paris. I could never have dreamt I'd one day have the privilege of working with these legends of the international art scene. Yet that's just what happened during my week at the Crazy Horse.

Below right: Here's something I wasn't expecting: like in factories many years ago, the Crazy Horse has got a time clock as well as matching time cards with the stage names of the girls on them. I wanted one too, and Andrée Deissenberg, the boss at the Crazy Horse, was only too happy to oblige. Yet, unlike the girls, I didn't get a new stage name. Conchita Wurst stayed Conchita Wurst, and that was fine by me.

Above left: This is a photo that by rights shouldn't exist. It shows me in a place that's off limits to men. It's the dressing room reserved for the 'Crazy Girls', although the term 'common room' might be a bit more like it. Before and after the shows, or if there's enough time between the two performances, this is where the 'Crazy Girls' hang out. They've made it as cosy as could be. There are only two men who are allowed in: Cyrill, the choreographer's assistant, and a barkeeper, whose job it is to make sure that no-one goes thirsty. As they were all agreed that I'd now qualified as a 'Crazy Girl', I was granted access to the room for the whole week. These women are among the best dancers in the world, but this is a room where they can be whatever they are outside of Crazy Horse: mothers, students, wives, party girls, divas. None of them pretended to be someone they weren't; they were all there for one another. I saw the way they cooked meals for each other, or baked cakes – and also how they looked out for each other like lionesses. It's like a family, an experience which welded us together. I'm sure that a large part of the Crazy Horse's success is down to the strong bonds between these women.

This was something which made me very happy: I got to go on a private guided tour of the Parisian National Opera, which has been home to some of the greatest theatre performances in the world over the last hundred years. I was allowed onto the roof as well, which has the most fantastic view over the rooftops of Paris.

Surprise! There were all keeping a secret from me at the Attitude Awards 2014 gala in the Banqueting House in Whitehall, London. Ana Matronic, the front-woman for the Scissor Sisters, was the hostess for the evening and she reminded me that the year before Daniel Radcliffe and Cher were included among the winners. Despite having no plans to emulate them, I was in for a surprise! The wonderful chef Nigella Lawson presented the 'Moment of the Year Prize' to me – and then it was time to party! I celebrated alongside Boy George and Ana, and felt happy knowing that all donations would be going to the Elton John AIDS Foundation.

If you think I've got a thing about shoes, you may just be right. No shoe shop is safe from me, and my shoe cupboard is bursting at the seams. Even so, I'm constantly on the lookout for new ones. Who knows what dark forces are at work here. When I'm not buying shoes, I love to photograph them. And there are some famous feet in the ones shown here. Write me if you can guess who's wearing them. Let's see if you're right!

Meeting with the Secretary-General of the United Nations Ban Ki-moon and his wife Yoo Soon-taek at the UN in Vienna. He is a wonderful speaker, especially when it comes to the exciting question of how each of us can contribute to a better world.

Preparing for the shoot of 'Heroes'
with my stylist Tom Reinberger.

CHAPTER TWENTY

JEAN PAUL
AND SISI

'Madame's a living legend;
I've seen so many idols fall
She is the greatest star of all.'
FROM THE MUSICAL *SUNSET BOULEVARD*

ARTE is a TV channel that owes its existence to Europe. It's one of the many things needed to make good neighbours out of former wartime enemies. My parents lived through the Cold War era. For them, just as for millions of other people, the fall of the Iron Curtain was a miracle. Yet the wars in former Yugoslavia and the conflict in Ukraine are a reminder that, despite epoch-making events behind us, we're still a long way away from being the 'United States of Europe'. ARTE was set up in 1992 in an effort to foster closer cultural ties between Germany and France, former enemies who had waged war against each other for centuries. I like ARTE and the kind of programmes it broadcasts, and so when they asked me whether I'd like to take part in the long-running documentary *Durch die Nacht mit ...*, I jumped at the chance.

The concept behind the show is simple: two prominent personalities – who sometimes don't even know each other – spend an evening together. If the chemistry is right, it's like a pleasant stroll around town, just like when you're out and about with a close friend. And the spectators can also take part. My *Durch die Nacht mit ...*was in Vienna, with Jean Paul Gaultier at my side. It was clear from the start that we'd have fun together.

'We'll do the Sisi Museum, for sure,' I announced, 'after all, he calls me his "young empress". And we can't miss the Prater public park. And a visit to a fashion school would be great. And a sausage stand is another must.'

I was buzzing with ideas. Having toured Europe, I was happy to be given this opportunity to show Jean Paul the best of my native city. We both opened our eyes wide with surprise when given details of the programme: a chauffeur-driven Rolls-Royce Silver Wraith stood ready to take us around the city like VIPs. Jean Paul let me in on the fact that he still suffered from nerves before every fashion show. The same went for many of his famous models, he confided.

'Madonna made two appearances, and she had the jitters on both occasions.'

'Me too,' I confessed. And I told him about how I felt the time the stage manager had called out 'She's fallen again'.

'And what about the critics?' I asked. Madonna's bodices had unleashed waves of enthusiasm among some critics while attracting bouts of head-shaking from others.

Jean Paul answered: 'I don't give a toss what they say,'

adding that they would never cause him to alter his style – which is lucky for us. The world would be a sad place if things were dictated by people who never like anything and always find something to grumble about. We've lived through times like those already, and they did us no good.

We arrived at the Sisi Museum. Housed in the imperial apartments of Vienna's Hofburg Palace, it's a place where you can immerse yourself in the life of the legendary Empress Elisabeth: from her happy childhood in Bavaria to her sudden engagement to the Emperor of Austria and finally to her murder in Geneva. Perhaps this was the first time a major contemporary designer had scrutinised her clothes in such detail. At any rate, Jean Paul was very taken with one of the dresses in the collection. A combination of black velvet and lace, it was the dress Sisi wore to her coronation as Queen of Hungary. He noted that the cut of the dress, with its open shoulders, would still today be modern and sexy.

'She had a tattoo, an anchor, on her shoulder,' I told him. 'Now everyone could see it. It was a scandal!'

Jean Paul laughed. 'Scandal is good! I'll make everything in my next collection open at the shoulder!'

He told me about the Cannes premiere of the movie *Saint Laurent*, in which my Austrian compatriot Helmut Berger plays the ageing fashion designer Yves Saint Laurent. Helmut's bisexuality had also caused a scandal – or what sceptics choose to call a scandal – and this prompted Jean Paul to tell me: 'What you're doing, you're doing for the freedom of men and women.'

Freedom. It's a big word. The Austrian constitution states that rule by force, show of force or despotism shall at all times be overridden by the binding force of law. This is intended to protect the basic rights that guarantee our freedom. Anyone familiar with Austrian history will know how arduous and rocky the path to these words was. This makes it all the more important to defend this freedom of ours. We must never tire in our efforts.

The car came to a stop. We'd arrived at the University of Applied Arts to visit a fashion class. The students were already waiting for us. After all, it's not every day that one of the world's top couturiers happens to drop in. Jean Paul Gaultier was full of praise for everything he saw. He broke the ice by letting everyone know about a mistake he'd once made as a young assistant to the great Pierre Cardin. Once you've made a small cut, it's easy to tear through natural fibres such as cotton, silk or linen. The same goes for synthetic fibres such as polyester and polyamide. This is an advantage, as everything can be done at speed, and, as we all know, time is money. Yet it's important to tear in the weft direction, otherwise you'll destroy the fabric.

'And that's just what I did,' Jean Paul told the students. 'A hellishly expensive material, and I ruined it. Pierre Cardin was furious. But the beginning is always hard.'

Tempted as we were to spend more time chatting with the students, we had an appointment with the Prater, the magnificent park without which no trip to Vienna would be complete. After a leisurely ride on the big wheel, we enjoyed a well-earned dinner. I invited Jean Paul to a restaurant boat moored on the Danube river. We both agreed that what really brings a city to life is a great river, as water always goes hand in hand with progress.

'This is something my grandmother often used to talk about,' I said. 'For her, it was the sea. "That's where new things come from," she'd say. I've never forgotten.'

We got round to talking about our parents and grandparents. Both of us had been fortunate enough to be born to tolerant fathers and mothers. It's something that can't be taken for granted. Parents often ask themselves where they went wrong if their daughter turns out to be lesbian or their son gay. Yet scientists proved long ago that there's no link whatsoever between upbringing and homosexuality. But how many people know that? It was reason enough for Jean Paul to come back to the Song Contest.

'Your victory was also our victory,' he told me, pointing out how important it is to bring the subject of homosexuality to centre stage. After all, the suicide rate among gay youth is four times as high as among heterosexuals. The ability of children and adolescents to come to terms with the challenges of their situation is greatly dependent on their environment.

'It's the same wherever you go, Austria, Europe, the whole world,' continued Jean Paul. 'That's why you also got points from the Russians.'

While we talked, we tucked in to my hometown's signature dish: Wiener schnitzel and potato salad. Having been restored to full strength thanks to the hearty meal, we watched an enjoyable performance by the choreographer Daniel Kok, and then brought the evening to a close at a sausage stand. In Vienna these places are an institution. Founded during the time of the imperial-royal monarchy to give war invalids an income, the sausage stand is an indispensable part of Viennese life. Of course, I insisted on placing our order myself: 'Cheese kransky, brown bread, hot mustard and sour gherkin. Plus two beers.'

Conchita Wurst at a sausage stand: that was too much for any passer-by to miss out on. Soon we were surrounded by onlookers, and then, all of a sudden, we were joined by three musicians with violins and a double bass, who played us a jazzed-up version of 'Rise Like a Phoenix'. Music really is everywhere in Vienna, even late at night at a sausage stand.

It was now time for us to bid each other farewell. I presented Jean Paul with an oversized print of our joint photo at the Life Ball. He was clearly delighted: *'C'est bon, regardez-là,'* he beamed. *'Merci mille fois!'*

I, too, felt very happy. I'd been given an opportunity to introduce my friend to Vienna in the way I like best: by presenting a city with its heart in the right place. I said goodbye in the traditional Viennese way, saying *'Pfiat di und baba'*, before disappearing into the night. Those words mean something like: 'Take care and see you soon!' See you soon, that's what we both wished.

CHAPTER TWENTY-ONE

US VERSUS ME

'So prepare for a chance of a lifetime
Be prepared for sensational news
A shining new era
Is tiptoeing nearer'

FROM THE MUSICAL *THE LION KING*

Politics, some say, is a dirty business. Politics, say others, has made central Europe into what all of us today are benefiting from: a union of countries that have gone seventy years without war. Leafing through the history books, you'll find no other era in which there was peace for so long. It seems that politics can work wonders, yet it can also frighten people or bore them, which is one of the reasons why so few young people turn out to vote. For me, politics is a necessity: if we want peace, acceptance and love, we can't wait for all these things to fall down from the sky. We have to do something about it ourselves, and that brings us to politics.

It's a word of Greek origin, and what I like about it is

that it focuses on the 'us', not the 'me'. Thankfully, there are many musicians who stand up for the 'us'. There's Bono from U2, who devotes himself to the fight against AIDS and debt relief for the Third World. And Bob Geldof, initiator of the Band Aid project and its worldwide Live Aid charity concerts. Then there's Elton John with his foundation, and Shakira with her Fundación Pies Descalzos for children in need.

On top of that, there are the pride parades, which advocate more 'us' and less 'me'. Be it Lesbian & Gay Pride, Gay & Lesbian Pride or Lesbian, Gay, Bisexual and Transgender Pride (LGBT Pride, for short), the focus is always on acceptance and love. On the night of 28 June 1969, the Stonewall Inn in New York's Greenwich Village was the scene of one of the then customary police raids against gays and lesbians. On this occasion, however, the outcome was not the usual one. Some of those about to be needlessly arrested fought back, with others joining in the protest.

Soon afterwards, the poet Allen Ginsberg, a leading figure of the famous Beat Generation, wrote the following words: 'It was about time we did something!' That doing something led to vigils and demonstrations. Soon the whole world was talking about the Stonewall uprising. That attempt to enforce democratic rights for all people gave rise to the pride parades. Today, they're colourful, festive events in which it's almost fashionable to take part, at least in the more enlightened corners of the globe. Yet the road there has been full of obstacles, and a glance at other countries around the world tells us that homophobia, exclusion and aggression are still commonplace. Even in what I just called the 'more enlightened corners of the globe', there are still traces of hatred against those who are 'different'. This is why I feel duty-bound to make it clear where I stand, no matter what the situation is. Both before and after the Eurovision Song Contest, I travelled all over the place to attend as many pride marches as possible.

I've been to Stockholm, Madrid, Antwerp, Manchester and many other cities. As is so often the case, it was Amsterdam that set the standard. It's a city we can all learn from. I'm always overwhelmed by just how many people turn out onto the street to fight for the cause, but in Amsterdam the whole city gets to its feet. Whether young or old, hetero or homo, it doesn't matter. Small children are there with their grandparents, dressed from head to toe in rainbow colours, the symbol of the movement. They sing, they dance, they're joyous, they share their excitement, they're not afraid of what's different, of what's new, they're refreshingly open. And that makes them successful: Amsterdam is one of Europe's top economic regions. This much is obvious: where there's fear, there's also economic stagnation. Where people are liberal and freedom-loving, there's success. Crises are overcome more easily, the future isn't viewed with foreboding.

Perhaps its waterside location, together with The Netherland's past as a seafaring nation, has made Amsterdam so open-minded. As a city, it has always been home to people who looked out beyond the horizon and welcomed in the rest of the world with open arms. New perspectives empowered them to create new possibilities. One of the things that sets the Amsterdam Pride apart is the kind of vehicles it uses. While other parades make their way through the city in cars and trucks, the city of canals favours transport on water. As usual, this year's boats sported large, imaginatively designed floats – so large, in fact, that I found it hard to believe they'd be able to manoeuvre their way through the narrow waterways. I then realised just how ingeniously everything had been constructed. In just a few quick movements, even the largest float could be collapsed to negotiate the next bridge. Apart from being fun to watch, it also demonstrated that, given sufficient imagination and inventiveness, any obstacle can be overcome.

For me, every pride festival is living proof that we're capable of achieving a whole host of positive things when we all pull in the same direction. Motivating people to do this is how I define politics. Every parade finishes with a closing event, and Amsterdam was no exception. The aim is that, alongside all the fun and entertainment, there should also be a message. On this occasion, the message addressed a question I've repeatedly asked myself: 'Will the day dawn when we no longer need parades? Will the day dawn when homosexuality is simply normal?' When couples have the confidence to walk through the streets hand in hand? When the church has no problem with those who are 'different'? When legislation allowing long prison sentences for homosexuals, as recently enacted by Ugandan president Yoweri Museveni, is unthinkable?

In Amsterdam, it's easy to forget that homosexuals and transgender people are still discriminated against, threatened and attacked. Other prides are less of a celebration and more of an outcry. 'Will the day dawn,' I wondered, 'when this outcry is no longer necessary?' I'm someone who despises violence. In the past, my response to death threats has often been somewhat flippant: 'OK, you can kill me, but you'll have to join the queue'. Yet, in reality, I'm greatly affected by such threats. I often have to force myself to read the newspapers or watch the news on TV, because we live in a world that risks going off the rails.

On his return from the International Space Station, the German astronaut Alexander Gerst spoke these heartfelt words: 'From up there in space, looking down on our little blue planet with its fragile atmosphere,' he said after 166 days in the ISS, 'it seems grotesque that people on Earth wage wars against each other and pollute the environment. We're surrounded by a black nothingness, and we know of no other place in the universe where we can live.'

His words reveal so much insight, an insight that not all of us have. I therefore see it as a duty to pass on experiences. Whether we're an astronaut or a musician, an actor or a model: if we're the ones in the limelight, we must face up to our responsibility to practise more 'us' and less 'me'. Then perhaps it really will dawn: the day when being different is no longer a cause for insults and violence.

CHAPTER TWENTY-TWO

IT'S ALL IN
THE DOING

'To fight for the right
Without question or pause'
FROM THE MUSICAL *THE MAN OF LA MANCHA*

There are some events to which I've become especially attached. One of them is *Light into Darkness*. The name says it all: *Light into Darkness* is Austria's biggest humanitarian relief campaign. In 1973, it began collecting donations for social projects, initially on the radio and then, five years later, also on TV. The show goes out on Christmas Eve and lasts fourteen hours, so it needs a good few hands on deck to answer the phone lines. I've been taking part for the past three years, and we always collect a considerable amount – almost 6 million euros in 2013. The same impressive total was reached in 2014. I've also released a cover of 'My Lights', the official song of *Light into Darkness*.

Actually doing something, taking part, being active and not sitting around complaining, is very important to me. Perhaps it's got to do with the fact that neither my mother nor my father ever sat there twiddling their thumbs doing nothing. Although I'm fond of a spot of *dolce far niente*, an old Italian expression meaning 'sweet idleness', that doesn't mean I want to make a virtue out of laziness. I'm happy when I've got something to do, especially if it's something worthwhile. I like to imagine a world in which everyone is able to do what they're good at and what gives them pleasure. I'm sure that would take humanity a big step forwards. What's needed is a range of options and an opportunity to take up those options. In my case, it was the fashion school in Graz, and my parents' willingness to support me meant I was able to attend. As I believe every human being has potential, I wish for everyone to have the chance to get ahead in life, wherever they come from and whoever they are.

This is why I was contacted by Green politician and Vice President of the EU Parliament Ulrike Lunacek. Together with MEPs from four different parties, Ulrike invited me to visit the European Parliament. The aim was to send out a message in support of the equality of lesbians, gays and bisexuals, as well as transgender and intersex individuals. As Ulrike herself is a lesbian, she knows exactly what she's talking about. Discrimination doesn't spare politicians – on the contrary. Although Germany has two prominent politicians who have publicly come out – Berlin's former mayor Klaus Wowereit and former German foreign minister Guido Westerwelle – it was a long road getting there. Wowereit was in fact one of the first major politicians world-wide to dare to utter in public the now iconic words, 'I'm gay, and proud of it.'

Yet if we take, say, the world of industry as an example,

then, with the exception of Apple CEO Tim Cook, there seem to be barely any homosexuals in the boardrooms. Even just in statistical terms, this can't be right. Gay people can lack the confidence to reveal their sexuality, for fear it will hinder their career prospects. The situation is even more blatant in football, where no active player at the top of the game has ever come out, for fear of turning fans into enemies. That's why I took a clear message with me to the European Parliament: quite simply, I expect greater commitment to the rights of homosexuals. 'It's your job,' I said, 'to fight for a functioning democracy and equal rights.'

CHAPTER TWENTY-THREE

GIRLS JUST WANT TO HAVE FUN – AND BOYS AS WELL!

'Welcome! You're a very nice surprise'

FROM THE MUSICAL *THE WOMAN IN WHITE*

Who was it that invented the selfie? I don't know, but I'd be pleased to receive your answers! Whoever it was deserves a medal, perhaps in the form of a digital camera. I can't say how many selfies I appear on, but I know one thing for sure: I'm a fan of these quick self-portraits, particularly as they get people chatting.

I recently checked into a famous hotel. A gentleman in a smart suit came round the corner, pulled out his smartphone, asked me for a selfie and then introduced himself as the establishment's chief press officer. 'Do you know,' he began, 'I was recently on holiday in Australia with my wife,' – excellent choice, I chipped in – 'and we went into this bar that looked like it might be nice.'

'Super. You've got to celebrate whenever you can.' I was in

the mood for a chat, and also keen to learn what happened next.

'Well, they were all partying as if there was no tomorrow. At some point, one of them asked us where we were from, and we replied...'

'Austria!'

'Correct! When they heard that, they all started flinging their arms around our necks! "You won, you won," they shouted. "*What* did we win?", I asked. There was more shouting and hugging. "The competition, you won the competition, the Song Contest, the one in Copenhagen!"'

I smiled. 'I believe I've heard of it.'

Suddenly, the man got serious. 'Do you know what I answered? That can't be the case, you must have got it wrong. We're from Austria! We never win anything!'

It seemed to me as if he was ashamed of the fact, and presumably he was. Unless it concerns ski jumping or the men's downhill, we Austrians have rather modest expectations of ourselves. I myself have repeatedly said: 'Before the Contest, I'd never won anything.' While we don't go round in sackcloth and ashes – nor is that necessary – a country with 8.5 million inhabitants is still just a small country. The metropolitan area of New York City is home to more than twice as many people as there are of us, while Tokyo has four times as many. On the other hand, we Austrians like to travel, with three out of four of us going abroad on holiday at least once a year. That could well be a record and goes to show that we look beyond our horizon. And so it is that we also find our way to Australia, to a bar where we learn something astonishing.

'I simply couldn't believe,' admitted the press officer, 'that an Austrian would be given such a rapturous welcome on the other side of the world. Would we do the same?'

On the evening in question, I left that question unanswered, but the correct response is, of course, 'Yes, we would'. I really like celebrating, and not just my own achievements, but also those of other people. How often have I heard the well-known saying 'business before pleasure'? I've never really understood it. What is it trying to tell me? Business and pleasure are two things that don't mix? So isn't it possible for work to be pleasure? It is for me. Then there's the time factor: we're supposed to do our work first and have our fun afterwards. But what if we're too tired by then, and don't feel like it anymore? Tough luck!

Following my encounter with the hotel press officer, these questions continued to occupy my mind for a while. Is it the reason why so many people go round with a worried look on their face? Because they've ruled pleasure out of their lives? Might hatred of others be a hatred of oneself, because life's no fun anymore? Isn't what we call entertainment just a way of passing time? Although it can be quite nice, it often leaves one feeling a bit flat afterwards. Are we just passing time, wasting time?

If I'm looking for pleasure, what gives me most enjoyment is being active. When my friend Nicole got married in 2011, there was, of course, a huge party. Yet, wanting to do something specially for her, I decided to sew her a wedding dress. It was really exciting, and I ended up being almost more nervous than she was. As it was supposed to be a surprise, she didn't get to try it on. And what if she didn't like it?

What woman wants to marry in a dress that isn't *the* dress? I designed a three-layered circle skirt à la Swinging Fifties. This requires a lot of material, and you have to sew long lengths of it. But, for Nicole's sake, I was happy to run my sewing machine almost red hot. Then came the moment of truth, when I presented it to her. Seeing her delight was like having a party of my own – and now the whole shebang could get underway. It's pretty clear I like having something to do when I'm celebrating, and if I can be creative at the same time, all the better. Perhaps this stems from the time when Conchita was married to Jacques Patriaque and – together with Urinella, the third member of the group – they would perform on stage.

For our performances, we were the Trio Infernale; in real life, we were the best of friends: Tom, Thomas and Philipp. Thomas and Philipp have been a couple for many years and are real role models to me. Despite having a lot of fun, we took our characters very seriously, constantly coming up with ideas to develop them. Urinella was a Viennese grande dame, who, although kind and likeable, was also capable of being the exact opposite. Somewhat cranky, wearing her heart on her sleeve, she was Mother Courage when it came to calling a spade a spade. Jacques, on the other hand – well, he was my husband – and the scenes from our marriage spoke volumes. He often went to spend a few weeks in New York, and, on returning, he'd be buzzing with ideas. At the same time as I was preparing for the Eurovision Song Contest, he was bringing out a new show, Europe's first Boylesque Festival, a quick-fire source of fun. *Girls just want to have fun – and boys as well!*

On one occasion, I had the pleasure of disguising myself so thoroughly that even my closest friends couldn't believe their eyes. It was Halloween, which is traditionally celebrated in Vienna with Miss Candy. She's a queen among drag queens, describing herself as lighter than a soufflé but tougher than Margaret Thatcher. The venue for the event was the U4. It's one of the best-known clubs in my adopted hometown – not because it was originally going to be a U-Bahn station but ended up becoming a club after the structural engineers got their calculations wrong, but because it's where any celebrity looking for a big night out in Vienna is sure to turn up at some time or other.

On the evening in question, the club was visited by the world-famous fashion designer Donatella Versace. Of course, everyone turned to gaze at her: her glamorous appearance, her long blonde hair, her slender waist, her bronzed skin. But she'd obviously been eating chilli peppers beforehand, the really hot Habanero ones. Anyone who spoke to her was sent packing in no uncertain terms, both in English and her strong native Calabrian dialect. And anyone looking to dance with her only got to see her claws. This was an evening on which it wasn't Prada the devil wore, but Versace, and there I was, having the time of my life. Because, underneath all the makeup, underneath the cheeks drawn back as if they'd been botoxed, it was me. It was like at Carnival time, when the mythical figure of the shapeshifter is celebrated up and down the land. I love this game of disguise, which dates back to the Germanic god Odin, who took on the shape of a bird or a snake.

I chose Donatella because I adore her, and because I was

able, through her, to give expression to my thoughts. It's the same with Conchita. The shapeshifter is there to give form to something that's missing. When things get all solemn and serious, and people run the risk of becoming too serious out of sheer awe at the importance of what's going on in the world around them, being unable to think for themselves, what's needed is something joyful that can surprise you, in the guise of a jester or clown. The Lakota Indians had their Heyoka, a man who always did the opposite of everything. When he said 'yes', he meant 'no', and when he said 'hello', he meant 'goodbye'. He sat on a horse the wrong way round, and, at rituals, he imitated the shaman by turning everything upside down. And what was the point of it all? To show the people that there was another side of the coin. That they should take a look at that side of things as well.

So while everyone was losing their head in revelry at Halloween, a stern shapeshifter disguised as Donatella was just what was needed. Because life is not a one-way street: there's always traffic in the opposite direction. Of course, there was a rapturous welcome for me when I finally revealed my true identity. The stunt had served its purpose. Despite all the fun we had, there was also a serious side. That's how I see it whenever Conchita takes to the stage: the audience enjoys the show, but if they can go home with a few new ideas – a memory stored in the back of their brain, ready to be brought out one day to prevent an insult, an act of discrimination or worse – then I've done my job. I believe in a strategy of small steps that lead ultimately to something much greater. If the constant drip, drip, drip can hollow out the rock, then every party, every celebration, every show is worthwhile.

CHAPTER TWENTY-FOUR

HOMEWARD BOUND

'I've seen blue skies
Through the tears in my eyes
And I realise I'm going home'
FROM THE MUSICAL *THE ROCKY HORROR PICTURE SHOW*

Vienna is now my home, my haven, to which I'm always glad to return. Yet Bad Mitterndorf, the scene of my childhood paradise, is the place that formed me. I turned my back on it at the age of fourteen, not entirely of my own free will, and now, a dozen years on, I made my way back there, once again not entirely of my own free will. Of course, I wanted to celebrate with the people who'd always supported me. I sensed a need to pay my respects to those who'd been on the edges of their seats in front of their TVs. And I wanted to say an especially warm thank you to the people who'd made their way from Bad Mitterndorf to Schwechat airport in Vienna to be there when I arrived. So far, so good. Nevertheless,

I found it difficult to get into my car to drive the less than 300 kilometres.

A trauma, I was recently informed by a friend who knows about these things, is a psychological condition that can periodically re-occur to cause the same symptoms as those originally experienced. That's how I felt at the thought of returning to the scene of my childhood. It was as if I'd been transformed back in time to age fourteen and was forced to listen once again to everything the less-than-enlightened people from my former hometown had had to say about me.

Although it wasn't the first time I'd travelled from Vienna to Bad Mitterndorf, going there as Conchita was a new experience for me. Despite having won the Eurovision Song Contest, I couldn't help asking myself: how will they receive me? What'll happen if the homophobes are still around? What if they disrupt the event? Perhaps they'll be so mad about my success they'll attack me? The worst possible scenarios kept going through my mind – I couldn't help it. Goethe's Faust speaks of 'two souls in my breast', and that's exactly how I felt that day. One of my souls wanted to return to the paradise of my childhood, relive the things that had been so worth experiencing: running along with happiness by my side on hot summer days, jumping across streams, coming home hot, hungry and thirsty and picking my favourite meal off the menu. My other soul remained cool and vigilant. Forget the romanticism, it told me, the past is the past, there's nothing left there for you to see, hear, feel or taste; there were many who didn't like you, just don't fool yourself that anything will have changed. But I've been invited, insisted my other soul, there's going to be a celebration, they're setting up a stage, the park's being closed off, I'll be performing with the band and singing with the local choir. They even want to make me an honorary citizen.

'The question is,' my distrustful soul went on, 'why did you need to win for them to do that? Don't you want everyone to be fairly treated, whoever they are and whatever they do?' That was a question to which I had no answer. Actually, I did have the answer, it was 'yes, I do,' but, at that moment, I wouldn't admit it. Otherwise I'd have had to cancel. I couldn't do that, nor did I want to.

Perhaps change comes about when you deliver the proof of something. In my early years, there were many people who thought that I, being gay, could never achieve anything in life. That's one of the many misjudgements most homosexuals suffer from. How is anyone who's so feeble and weak ever going to make it? But perhaps the boneheads will change their attitude once the unimaginable happens? 'Oops! I was wrong. Perhaps I should reconsider?' Granted, that sounds pretty naive, like wishful thinking. Then again, nothing ventured, nothing gained. That was as true in this case as in any other sphere of life, and it became my main reason for tackling one of the most difficult days in my life: returning to Bad Mitterndorf.

I was received like a queen, a president, a superstar. The whole town turned out, and those in charge did everything to make me feel at home. Unfortunately, as humans we often have a distorted perception of reality: we hear the loudmouths, even when they're in the minority, and forget that the majority hold a different opinion. You can't see people who are in the dark, so the saying goes – and if the majority fail to open their mouths, they remain in the dark. On the day I returned to Bad

Mitterndorf, things were different: now it was the majority that were most visible – and they liked me. The boneheads stayed at home and vented their frustration on the internet. I could see, hear, feel and taste that the people who'd turned out were honestly proud of me, accepted me as a human being and not as the one who was 'different'. Even so, I kept having to get a grip on myself, because my vigilant soul wouldn't allow me to relax, even though the thousands of photos taken that day tell a different story.

It was a rollercoaster ride, a flood of constantly changing emotions that sometimes threatened to drown me, like when I took to the stage with my childhood friend Kristin and we sang the song that many years before had transported us off to another and, as we thought, better world: 'California Dreamin'' by the The Mamas and the Papas. The words 'I could leave today, California dreamin', on such a winter's day' had become our mantra; I could leave today, a sentence I'd clung on to.

Then there was another, joyful moment I could never have dreamt of: me on stage with my grandmother. Isn't life crazy? She'd been such a huge influence, both before and after my coming-out. Her life motto isn't criticism, but openness, so I was deeply moved to have the honour of standing next to her while the spectators applauded.

The second song I sang that day, accompanied by my cousins on piano, was 'Unbreakable'. It's another anthem of mine. 'She finds it hard to trust someone, she's heard the words cause they've all been sung, she's the girl in the corner.' As I sang, I was thinking to myself: who knows whether, among all the spectators out there, there isn't a boy or a girl who's being forced into the corner because they're different and can't find their way in the world. How would I have felt if a Conchita had turned up one day, cheered on by the masses? What impression would it have left on me? How much stronger would I have felt afterwards?

Since I'm now aware of how important role models are, I identify even more strongly with outsiders as soon as I take to the stage. On this day, I was thinking of all the little Toms who exist just as much today as they did back then, and who perhaps went home with a stronger sense of self-belief after the concert. Next up was the song 'That's What I Am', performed together with the local choir in traditional costume, and, of course, 'Rise Like a Phoenix', with the accompaniment of the town band. After that, I was awarded my honorary citizenship by the mayor, Dr Karl Kaniak. By that point, I definitely thought I must be dreaming. The town had awarded two honorary citizenships to date, one to the popular author Hans Fraungruber and the other to skiing pioneer Theodor Karl Holl – and now me, Conchita Wurst, the bearded female singer, drag queen, and political activist. Unbelievable!

And as if that wasn't enough, the town even went one better: a commemorative plaque was to be erected in the town centre, bearing the words I spoke after my victory in Copenhagen: 'This night is dedicated to everyone who believes in a future of peace and freedom. You know who you are – we are unity and we are unstoppable'.

My parents' restaurant is always a busy place, as they're wonderful hosts. Yet the Song Contest took things to a new level, and there were now people everywhere. Fortunately, my mother has her kitchen under perfect control, while my father is virtually unflappable. As long as he still has time for his hobby – making ornate cribs – he can keep things running even when the place is bursting at the seams. My mother told me that Conchita fans from Mexico and other parts of the world had travelled to Bad Mitterndorf to visit the birthplace, *la casa natal, la maison natale, la casa natia* of Ms Wurst – only to learn that I'd actually been born a few hundred kilometres further away. 'They had a good time anyway,' said my mother, and I bet they also enjoyed their food.

When I returned to Vienna some time later, my head was still spinning with all the things I'd just experienced. On the other hand, the two souls in my breast had calmed down. My vigilant, cool soul was soothed by the warmth shown to me by the people of Bad Mitterndorf, while the soul that dreamt of my childhood paradise was exhausted, yet happy. At some point during all the goings-on, I'd said, 'Childhood, that was the time before I went to school,' and who's to say how many of today's children feel the same, because, a few days later, it was once again time for the loudmouths to raise their ugly voices, their responses being inevitable – ranging from, 'I'm off, Bad Mitterndorf will never see me again', to this message in misspelt Styrian dialect: *'Es is jo eh scho so zum schama gwesen das des objekt zum contest hod foan derfm* (Why did we have that "thing" representing us at the ESC? What a bloody disgrace!).'

Too bad. If Conchita Wurst didn't polarise opinion, what'd be the point of her? It's only by giving the loudmouths something to mouth off about that we know they still exist, and that our mission hasn't yet been accomplished.

CHAPTER TWENTY-FIVE

KIDS? KIDS!

'When we're in public together,
I hear society moan'

FROM THE MUSICAL *CABARET*

'If I was a hetero, you'd be the woman I'd want to have children with.'

It's not the kind of thing you can say to just any woman. But to my friend Anja, I can. She's heard me say it loads of times. Anja is the cousin of Matthias, my brilliant hair stylist, and whenever she meets my mother, she greets her with the words, 'Hello, mother-in-law!' Anja will get married one day, and then she'll be able to say the same words to her real mother-in-law. But, until that day comes, we'll continue to enjoy our little joke. It's when you start exploring how things are in reality that it turns more serious. The difference between tolerance and acceptance is often reflected in the debate over children. Although many people are now tolerant of gays and lesbians, accepting them as parents is another matter. One of the most harmless questions is 'How on earth is that supposed to work?' This is followed by: 'But which of you is *really* the child's mother or father?' Then there's 'It can't work', which raises doubts about the child's upbringing. Finally, there's 'God forbids it', an expression of the fundamentalist 'no'.

According to an opinion poll for the European Commission, Austria is one of Europe's most tolerant countries when it comes to gays and lesbians, with as many as forty-nine per cent of my compatriots being in favour of same-sex marriage, while forty-four per cent have nothing against child adoption by same-sex couples. Homosexual couples have been allowed to marry since 2010 – not in church, of course, but at least at a registry office. The presiding official, however, doesn't utter the standard, 'I hereby pronounce you husband and wife'. Instead, the marriage becomes lawful once the couple have signed their names in the book. For some, this difference in procedure is irrelevant, but others take a different view.

Joint adoption has been allowed since 2013. 'Rainbow family' is the colloquially used term, even in cases where a gay or lesbian couple have gone down the route of artificial insemination in order to fulfil their wish for a child. Incidentally, such children normally do very well. More than that, they often do better than in other families. Why is this the case? The reason is that, in a rainbow family, children don't just 'happen'. They're genuinely wanted, because there are many hurdles to overcome, at both the bureaucratic and social level. It's something that only people who really want a child are ready to go through.

And what about me? I can't say. Whenever I meet Anja,

we give each other a hug, and I tell her with a smile, 'If I was hetero, you'd be the woman I'd want to have children with.' We have a laugh about it, while at the same time sensing the poignancy of it all, because, one of these days, when Anja gets married, the sentence will have to be struck from my vocabulary.

CHAPTER TWENTY-SIX

PIERRE AND GILLES

'Paris loves lovers, for lovers it's heaven above
Paris tells lovers, love is supreme, wake up your
dream and make love'

FROM THE MUSICAL *SILK STOCKINGS*

Paris had me again. To be honest, Paris always will. Vienna
is my home, I like the energy of London, while Copenhagen
signifies freedom. But it's Paris that stands for love. Haute
Couture Week was coming to a close, and all of us were still
under tremendous pressure. Now France's *Vogue* magazine
had invited me to its gala dinner, where Jean Paul Gaultier
introduced me to his boyfriend, Konstantinos Katalakinos.
Ever the romantic, I immediately wanted to know where the
two of them had met. Jean Paul smiled. 'I suppose,' he began,
'it was when I invited him to my show.'

'And that was it? Come on, couldn't you come up with
something more original than that?'

149

Jean Paul shrugged his shoulders impishly. 'But that's how it was.'

'That one can only work when your name is Gaultier!'

'What was I supposed to do, my young empress? I didn't have anything else up my sleeve. He didn't even know I was there!'

'Wait a minute!' Konstantinos chipped in. 'That's not true. You were surrounded by people, all of them talking to you at the same time ...'

I laughed. Here I was again with the most exciting fashion designer of our age, and it was as if we saw each other every day. Despite that, I'd shocked even myself with my boldness, not that it seemed to bother Jean Paul. And as Conchita is an incredibly nosy lady, the conversation continued in the same vein.

'What about you, Konstantinos,' I went on. 'What do you do when you're not looking glamorous at gala dinners?'

Of course, I knew he worked as a model and stylist, but his reply certainly livened up the conversation. 'I'm Jean Paul's boyfriend,' he said. 'That's work enough.'

We talked about the future, and that meant: Crazy Horse. A name to make the heart skip a beat. It's one of the last of the famous revue theatres in the city of light, which blazed a trail with the Moulin Rouge, the Lido, the Paradis Latin and the Folies Bergère. Situated in the best part of town on Avenue George V, the Crazy Horse was established in the early 1950s by Alain Bernardin. Today, the director is Andrée Deissenberg. I'd already met her and had been amazed to find that I could speak German with her.

Andrée had laughed. '"*Franchouillard*", is what the

customers say, meaning "typically French": that's the Crazy Horse. Not even a German director can change that.' She told me about how she'd worked twelve years at the Cirque du Soleil, the world-famous circus founded over thirty years ago and now run by the Canadian street artist Guy Laliberté. 'You know, it's got neither a circus ring nor performing animals. Instead, it has these sensual, crazy, breathtaking shows. We were forever on tour, and travelled halfway round the world. It was there that I learned show business from the bottom up.'

I wanted to know what role a revue theatre could play in an age when eroticism is often just a mouse click away. How do you create a scintillating atmosphere when people have already seen everything? I liked what Andrée had to say in reply: 'With imagination. We show them that women are art. And that's where you come in.'

The Crazy Horse regularly puts on special shows featuring illustrious guests such as the fashion icon Dita von Teese and the French character actress Clotilde Courau. But something it had never had before was a bearded and very feminine woman, *barbu et très féminin*, as the French media later put it. Jean Paul Gaultier would lend me a dress, and I'd have three other exceptional costumes at my disposal. Andrée was able to dispel my greatest fear: 'But I'm not a dancer!'

'Oh, we've already got enough of those. And they're good, believe me!'

Andrée was right. Anyone looking to succeed as a dancer at the Crazy Horse needs classical ballet or dance training. That's followed by three months of further intensive training, and only then is the stage open for performers such as Viola

Waterloo, Taïna de Bermudes, Lava Stratosphere, Loa Vahina and Jade Or. These are the stage names of the dancers, all of whom are between 168 cm and 172 cm tall. As Andrée was giving me a tour of the theatre, we happened to walk past an old-fashioned looking machine.

'What's that?' I asked.

'Our time clock.'

A time clock? That's what they used to have in factories. When the workers turned up for the start of their shift, they inserted their time card into a kind of box, which then stamped the card with their time of arrival. They did the same before going home. At the end of the month, the card was sent to the accounts department, which calculated the number of hours worked. Although the time clock has survived in electronic form, I wouldn't have expected to find a place like the Crazy Horse still using a machine from such a bygone age.

'Our girls would revolt if we got rid of the time clock,' smiled Andrée.

'Do I get my own time card?'

'Of course you do. With your stage name on it.' Andrée pointed to a rack next to the clock, in which all the cards were neatly arranged. 'Afterwards you put your card in there. But you won't need an extra name like Baby Light or Mika Do – you're Conchita. Why bother changing it?'

'That's fine with me, as long as I get my card.' I'd never had a time card in my life, and in all probability, I'll never be given one again. I liked these little idiosyncrasies of the Crazy Horse, which recalled the great days of revue theatre.

'The era of the nightclub began in the twentieth century,'

explained Andrée. 'The Kit Kat Klub in New York. The Stardust Hotel in Las Vegas. The Palladium in London, and, of course, the Lido in Paris. We're keeping a tradition alive, and our guests appreciate that.'

She showed me the ballroom, in which I sensed an atmosphere of sensually provocative shows, a place that was made for the night. Intimate, yet not vulgar. Comfortable armchairs around narrow tables, lacquered wood and red velvet. My heart, which is in love with night revues, started to pound.

'There are two shows an evening, aren't there?' I asked.

'That's right. It'll be marvellous, I promise you. But also exhausting.'

She wasn't wrong. I travelled frequently to Paris to rehearse with the dancers. Each time I was fascinated by their musicality, movement, litheness and sensuality. What had Andrée said? 'We show that women are art.' These dancers were the living proof of her words. And there was I in their midst, a man who loves women, yet doesn't desire them – that was something really exceptional, for the girls as well. They put their body on display, and even though it's always artistically illuminated, subtly veiled in vital places, with more being hidden than shown, it's still a naked body. I admired their beauty without allowing myself to be seduced by it. We had a lot of fun together, totally free of any deeper meaning. I learned a lot, and I got to collaborate with two legends: Pierre and Gilles.

The photographer Pierre Commoy and the painter Gilles Blanchard are the talented men responsible for the stage sets at the Crazy Horse. Having long been an admirer of their work, I would never have dreamt I'd one day be collaborating with them. For more than forty years, they've been surprising the international art scene with their lavish portraits in front of a three-dimensional backdrop. Be it Marc Almond from Soft Cell, Khaled, the King of Raï, the French superstars Catherine Deneuve and Serge Gainsbourg, Madonna or Paloma Picasso, they've all posed for Pierre and Gilles. And now it was my turn.

I'd been standing in the same pose for almost an hour, with wide-outstretched arms, which were by now burning like fire. *'Ne bouge pas!'* don't move, commanded Pierre for the umpteenth time. Millimetre by millimetre, they arranged every single strand of my hair, while I distracted myself from the pain by letting my eyes wander around the fabulous cave the two of them called their studio. I was allowed to move my eyes, and what they saw would have delighted little Tom, too. Pierre and Gilles live in a house on the edge of Paris, and on entering, you walk straight into a museum. It's not one that specialises in contemporary art or the Old Masters. Instead, it's a museum of unusual everyday art, an oasis of trashy cultural phenomena from past and present. Marvel Comics action figures are lined up alongside Mexican chandelier advertisements. Popeye can be seen making himself comfortable on a Mayan Sun-patterned tablecloth. In the corner, a life-size Michael Jackson in synthetic resin is flirting with Batman. Jade elephants, musical instruments, monstrous Dino-Riders from the 1990s, Surmese lip plates, trumpet alarm clocks from the 1920s. What struck a neat freak like me, of course, was how everything was so nicely arranged and in perfect condition – including in the cellar, down into which this orgy of rarities seamlessly continued. This was a bit of luck, since all of my looking around and marvelling enabled me to survive the crucifixion scene.

'*Bouge pas!*' This time it was Gilles. Don't move! He manipulated the sash on my dress into precise shapes, with the accuracy of a man accustomed to meticulous craftsmanship. He then took each of my fingers and placed them in the desired positions. '*Un centimètre à gauche, s'il vous plaît. Seulement un, Madame, pas deux!*' One centimetre to the left, please. Not two, just one!

Despite the pain – my arms were now trembling – I'd immediately taken to both of them. I love people who are passionate about what they do. That should be our goal. Not doing things because they need doing. But doing them with enthusiasm, zeal and commitment. Of course, Pierre and Gilles are successful. Their work adorns front pages, they have exhibitions in Seoul, Shanghai, Berlin and Paris, they work for the Crazy Horse and the fashion industry – but they'd still do what they do even if no-one was interested. They do their work because they enjoy taking their art to a deeper level. For me, that's the key to success. My experience with *Starmania* and the manufactured band jetzt anders! taught me to be suspicious of success that's planned out in advance. The organisers might get lucky and create something that really does contain a spark of passion, in which case it might be successful. Usually, however, that isn't the case. You can't plan success in the same way you plan a journey. Success happens when we follow our heart, and that means finding out what we enjoy doing. And then designing a strategy. How can I do more of what I enjoy doing? How can I build on what I enjoy doing? How can I get good at it? When I say 'good', I mean better than the rest.

That's what Pierre and Gilles did, and they became legends. Pierre loved photography, while Gilles loved illustration. He began to overpaint Pierre's portraits. Together they turned it into an art form. I find this sort of dedication both motivating and inspiring. That day, as I spent half an eternity in the same pose, with outstretched arms and moving my fingers centimetre by centimetre – *'un, pas deux'* – it became clear to me that, at that moment in time, there was nothing, absolutely nothing in the world I'd rather be doing. That's how I managed to maintain the same uncomfortable posture, despite my body's protestations. When it was all over, I knew: you can always do a little bit more than you think. During the week I spent doing the shows at the Crazy Horse, this realisation was a great help to me.

CHAPTER TWENTY-SEVEN

CRAZY HORSE

'The French are glad to die for love'

FROM THE MUSICAL *GENTLEMEN PREFER BLONDS*

I couldn't have chosen two more dissimilar sets if I'd wanted to. On Saturday evening, I took to the stage on the German TV show *Wetten, dass..?* for the world premiere of my new song 'Heroes'. Less than twelve hours later, I was on another stage, this time in Paris at 12 Avenue George V, wearing a skin-tight Gaultier dress, surrounded by the city's most beautiful dancers. It was a magical moment. Pierre and Gilles had created a set to die for, the dancers were in top form, and I could sense the energy that always runs through my body whenever I'm on stage. A 'stage hog' is a somewhat disparaging term for an artist who exists for the moments they're performing live in front of the world. That's me. The live show is the king of gigs. Anything can happen, nothing can be depended on. When we're used to a world where seemingly nothing is left to chance, the live show is both a challenge and a thrill. Of course, we'd practised and rehearsed over and over again. Yet when the curtain goes up and the audience collectively hold their breath in anticipation, the only thing that counts is the moment at which we all give it our best. That's the point at which I sense life coursing through my veins, feel the energy I can give, and the energy I get back in return.

Without a doubt, the applause of the audience is our greatest reward. 'Dedicated to amazement' are the words emblazoned in gold letters on a dark blue background in Berlin's Jardin de Plaisanterie, today's Wintergarten Varieté. Spectators at circuses are greeted with the motto 'Your favour is our striving', and that's the magic of the live show: no tricks, no playback, no false floor and no safety net, yet still giving the audience an experience they'll remember for a long time to come. Seen in this light, my week at the Crazy Horse was incredibly exciting. Like at Kitty Willenbruch's burlesque revue in Vienna, I returned to being a night worker on the late shift. I loved it! The night's not just there for sleeping – it's also there for partying! After all those weeks of work on 'Heroes', all the long hours in the film studio, political appearances and interview marathons, it was a joy to finally get back to where it had all begun: on stage, the place that opens up a whole new universe for us.

Live!

Pure adrenaline!

Curtain up at the Crazy Horse!

We played two shows a day, and any of us whose muscles weren't aching afterwards must have been doing something wrong. Our last performance of the day behind us, the evening was still far from over. We partied and discussed the things we wanted to get better in the next show. By the time I got to bed, it wasn't long before dawn. I'd often reflect on what the Paris of the 1920s and 1930s must have been like, a time when the live show was one of people's main pleasures. A time when, evening after evening, thousands used to flock to the Casino de Paris or Théâtre des Champs-Élysées to celebrate the golden age of French variété. To see the great clown Grock, or Josephine Baker, who used to shock all the visitors to the Folies Bergère by wearing a skirt made entirely of bananas. As is often the case, past times are forgotten times. So I was aware that, with our show, we were helping to keep alive the tradition of a golden era.

On entering my hotel at the crack of dawn, I would look out towards the Champ de Mars, where the Eiffel Tower was reflecting the sun's first rays. For me, that iconic structure is a promise that Paris will always remain Paris, a place where, even in the twenty-first century, a revue show can still captivate an audience. I could already sense the thrill of those hours before a performance reawakening inside me. On my way to the hotel, someone had sprayed *'Pour l'éternité'*, for all eternity, on the wall of a house, and the words were still imprinted on my mind. I could stay here and play on forever, they seemed to be telling me. But then I closed the hotel door behind me and rested before my next show, and then the next one, and the next one – and so it went on for a wonderful week, but alas not for all eternity. Because there were new challenges awaiting me, relating to a video with a simple title: 'Heroes'.

CHAPTER TWENTY-EIGHT

HEROES

'Gonna fly now, flying high now'

FROM THE MUSICAL *ROCKY*

Six months isn't a long time in terms of the history of the world. Yet my fans, thinking in terms of the history of Conchita Wurst, were beginning to demand: When are you going to bring out your new song?

I could only ask them to be patient, because I wanted the best song for them, plus a wonderful video. For someone like me, born in the late 1980s, song and video belong inseparably together, even though the age of the music video had begun only a few years before I was born. I'd grown up watching MTV, and took a big interest in hit lists such as MTV's *100 Greatest Music Videos Ever Made* and *TMF's Ultimate 50 Videos You Must See* by The Music Factory TV channel. I can remember one of the first masterpieces, 'Sledgehammer' by Peter Gabriel, which involved the people from Aardman Animations, who were later to become world-famous with the *Wallace and Gromit* movies. And Madonna's 'Papa Don't Preach', which was made by Hollywood director James Foley with one of the best ever cameramen in the business, Michael Ballhaus. Music videos like these were milestones and have rarely been surpassed by any that came before or after them.

I was clear in my mind that, if I was going to sing about dancing in the eye of a hurricane, I wanted to see a shot of it. So I met up with Gerhard Gutscher's video artists at the Vienna Sound Vienna Light studios, who had already done work for Cher, Jermaine Jackson, Anastacia, John Cleese, Grace Jones and Nigel Kennedy. I told them about the images I had in my head. A synaesthete is the name given to people like me, people who see pictures when they listen to music. The more emotional my reaction is to a piece of music, the stronger my synaesthesia becomes. That's because emotions add to the visual response. Although it's essentially a positive thing, it can sometimes also be stressful, as the pictures are always extremely vivid. And that's how it was when my inner eye visualised the first sequences of the video. Intensely realistic pictures shot through my brain as I was going down the steps at an underground station. Once again, I had to be careful not to stumble. On the other hand, I never have to worry that the pictures in my head will suddenly go away, like ideas that have scarcely appeared before they disappear again. The pictures stay on, yet they also present themselves as an obligation: work with us, they say. Make something out of us.

I used to listen to music while sewing. It allowed me to transfer the pictures directly from my head to the design

I was creating. The images that surfaced in my mind were never ones I'd seen before. Likewise, there are generations of people who can all remember exactly the same picture. This phenomenon was illustrated years ago at an exhibition by the artist Michael Schirner. His 'Pictures in our Minds' series showed photos that everyone knew. The trick was that not one of the photos was actually on view. Instead, visitors were presented with black panels and white writing: 'Willy Brandt kneeling at the monument to the victims of the Warsaw Ghetto Uprising', 'East German policeman jumping over barbed wire into the West as the Berlin Wall is being built', 'Footprint of the first man on the moon'. Every visitor to the exhibition immediately had the picture in their head, because they'd seen it so often. A similar exhibition today would offer us pictures with titles such as 'Collapse of the World Trade Center' or 'Russian President Vladimir Putin topless while fishing'. These are pictures that have become common property. Yet if your aim is to create a stand-out video, they're pictures you'd do well to avoid.

So I rely on the images from my synaesthesia, even if they do cause me to take the odd fall. The pictures I see are ones that have never been seen by anyone before. So how am I supposed to communicate them? The director Steven Spielberg once spoke the following words about the art of filmmaking: 'It's twenty per cent imagination and eighty per cent presentation'. And the creator of *E.T.*, *Jurassic Park*, *Men in Black*, *Indiana Jones* and *Schindler's List* is someone who really ought to know. I spoke in depth to the people from the Vienna Sound Vienna Light studios about all the things I'd seen, and we discussed how to transfer my mental pictures to the screen.

Ultimately, 'Heroes' is about how each one of us can be a hero in our own day-to-day life, and about freedom of choice: we ourselves choose the path we take and whether that path is paved with hate, violence and hostility, or with love, acceptance and joy. I often hear how it's circumstances that turn a person into a murderer, a criminal, a homophobe or a corrupt politician. Yet aren't these just convenient excuses we use to hide from our own responsibility? All those who post messages like 'Rot in hell' on my Facebook account have made their decision. I've made mine, too, and I've chosen not hate, but love. I've chosen 'we can be so beautiful'. And I'm certain that, at the end of the day, it's the only option open to humankind. The world is home to over seven billion people, and that number is set to rise much higher in the coming years. The day is likely to dawn when no wall is high enough to separate rich from poor, black from white, homo from hetero. If we can accept each other in a spirit of love, we'll make it. Until that day comes, the warlords and the dictators, the oppressors and the despots will fight their last battles. Ultimately, they'll have no chance. No-one can stop us. Our love is stronger than their hate.

CHAPTER TWENTY-NINE

OF CHANCELLORS, PRESIDENTS AND SECRETARIES-GENERAL

'The overture is about to start,
You cross your fingers and hold your heart,
It's curtain time and away we go!'

FROM THE MUSICAL *KISS ME, KATE*

We are unstoppable, *wir sind nicht zu stoppen, nous sommes imparable, somos imparables* – my dream has become a reality. My words, our slogan, went out into the world, found an audience, spread like wildfire. Those words gave hope to unheard voices, they woke the sleeping, united the strong. They also annoyed the homophobes, the misanthropes, the egoists. On the evening of 10 May 2014, I had no time for them, but that's now changed. We reach out our hand. We'll take everyone on board. It's never too late to feel love.

When I close my eyes, I dream of a Europe of friends. So far, the Union is just an association of states in which the people from one country still know little about the people from the other countries. Of course, it would be wrong to believe that friendship is something that can happen overnight. It would be wrong to believe that the process can proceed without setbacks. It would be wrong to believe that the diehards won't resist. That's why, at a time when others wanted to see me in a music studio, I was embarking on a journey to carry my message out into the world. Just days after the Eurovision Song Contest, I met with the Austrian Chancellor Werner Faymann and Culture Secretary Josef Ostermayer. Once again, I asked myself: how is this possible? How can someone from Bad Mitterndorf debate with those in power?

Yet it turned out that many of the people I spoke to are themselves from the provinces. Former US President Bill Clinton, a firm favourite at the Vienna Life Ball, hails from the small town of Hope in Arkansas. Mayor of Vienna Michael Häupl, who made me a Golden Standard Bearer of the City of Vienna for 'respect and coexistence', was born in Altlengbach, a village with only 2,700 inhabitants. Ban Ki-moon, former Foreign Minister of South Korea and now Secretary-General of the United Nations, grew up in the countryside. Ulrike Lunacek, Vice President of the European Parliament, comes from Krems on the Danube, and Heinz Fischer, the Austrian President, is a native of Graz, the capital of the Austrian state of Styria.

There are always going to be exceptions to the rule. To all those who feel voiceless because they're far away from the global centres of power, I say: wherever we come from, let's do our bit to make this world a better place! We can be heroes. We just need to want it.

CHAPTER THIRTY

CONCHITA GOES BANKING

'I place my faith in you,
I do believe'

FROM THE MUSICAL *SCARLET PIMPERNEL*

If there's been one word in recent years that's come to epitomise scandalous conduct, it's *banking*. This contrasts with what I learnt at fashion school, which prepared us for a level of self-reliance that would be impossible without the services of a bank. During my schooldays, I had enjoyed researching the history of it all. How many people know that the concept of the trading exchange was born 600 years ago, in a house in Wollestraat in Bruges? Back in the fourteenth century, what enabled this Flemish town to stand out from the other European trading centres was one key advantage it had over Leipzig, Frankfurt, Amsterdam and Paris: an inn run by the van de Beurse family. The family's coat of arms consisted of three leather purses, and not without reason: this was a place where there was good business to be done.

It was somewhere that people traded not in goods, but in information. Who was buying or selling where, what and at what price? This was the idea of the van de Beurse family, and it was a successful one. Theirs was a place where traders could do business without needing to have their wares physically with them. Apart from that, the van de Beurse inn served up Flemish specialities, such as rabbit stew with plums and steamed eel in chervil sauce – and so the trading exchange was born.

Back at fashion school, I had no idea that, just a few years later, I'd be running a company of my own, a company that now employs over a dozen people. With this responsibility resting on my shoulders, I was forced to address some entirely new questions: how do I finance my business? How can I be a dependable employer for my employees? These were the questions that confronted me in the months after the Eurovision Song Contest. To begin with, we worked in two small rooms in the 20th district of Vienna, where we were quite literally stepping on each other's toes. With five of us all on the phone at the same time, which was frequently the case, you could hardly hear your own voice. We held our meetings across the counter in a small kitchen. My seat was on the stool in the corner, always within easy reach of the coffee machine. It was here that we discussed and planned until late into the night. One thing was clear: we were going to grow, and if you're going to grow, you'll need a new home.

Our new home was an office close to Vienna's Millennium Tower, spread out over two floors, with enough space for everyone. The conference room alone is as big as our old office, and we've got a kitchen, where we cook together once a week. All of this required a solid financial basis. So, on top of my stage work, interviews and travels around Europe, I also began to have dealings with bankers, the very people who in recent years took the whole world to the brink of disaster. I must admit I was sceptical. But then I learnt that not all bankers are the same. The bankers I got to do business with were not the same as the ones in *The Wolf of Wall Street*. They were more in line with the old-fashioned image of the bank manager concerned with building up a solid business relationship with his clients.

When Bank Austria asked me whether I could see myself working more closely with them, I was curious to see what they had in mind. The bank employs more than 7,000 people, and since becoming an employer myself, I now see such figures from a new perspective. In this case, 7,000 employees meant 7,000 individual destinies to shape. What finally won me over was when we talked about the slogan for our cooperation: 'Working together for a better togetherness'. This spoke to me from the heart. I believe that, while we as individuals can achieve only little, we as a team can achieve a great deal. As long as you're on the right track, there's nothing else that can go wrong. The bank was planning a cashback system that rewards customers with automatic permanent discounts.

'Reminds me of when I used to collect money-off coupons with my mother,' I said.

'The only difference is that it's now all automatic,' came the reply.

This brought us to the crux of the matter. Anyone in Austria using their bank card to pay for goods or services from a partner of Bank Austria will get cash back every month as a reward. In addition, there's an automatic donation to a social project as part of 'Working together for a better togetherness'. For me, this closed the circle. Our aim should not be to have, have, have, but to share wherever possible. Of course, it felt a little strange seeing my own face on a bank card and having cardboard effigies of myself at bank branches across the country. 'Conchita goes banking' wasn't exactly what people had expected from me. Then again, neither was seeing me as a businesswoman. I thought back to when I'd left home as a fourteen-year-old to go down a route that wasn't available where I lived. Setting up my own business belonged in the same category. So it was important to think back to what had driven me then: curiosity, together with love as the basic essence of everything. It's the same today, and it'll be the same tomorrow – and the next day, and the next.

CHAPTER THIRTY-ONE

THE ROAD AHEAD

'So promise me only one thing, would you?'

FROM THE MUSICAL *PROMISES, PROMISES*

Zoila Augusta Emperatriz Chavarri del Castillo, known as Yma Sumac, is a female singer I continue to revere even after her death. Born in Peru, she lived for a long time in the Andes, the longest and second-highest chain of mountains in the world. People live high up in this tierra nevada – the land of snow – at altitudes of 4,500 metres and above. Legend has it that it was the thin air up there that gave Yma's voice its amazing quality. For her, five octaves was nothing, which prompted the US talk show host David Letterman to describe Yma as 'a miracle of nature'. Yma herself claimed simply to have the lung capacity of someone who lives in the Andes, which happened to be greater than that of other people. Her breakthrough wasn't long in coming. Soon her name was on everyone's lips, with a string of artists being inspired by the so-called Nightingale of the Andes. The Coen brothers used her music for their movie *The Big Lebowski*, while her phenomenal voice also featured in the Cirque du Soleil show *Quidam*.

Yma's reputation even made it into the German-speaking world when her song 'Xtabay' was used in the film *The Austrian Method*. Why am I telling you all this? Because singing is going to carry on being one of my most passionate endeavours in the future, and I'll revel in upholding the art of the female singers I admire. Whenever I get the chance to meet such artists personally, my heart beats even faster. That's what it was like when I had the privilege to meet María de los Ángeles Santamaría Espinosa, who in 1968 became the first Spaniard to win the Eurovision Song Contest, under her stage name Massiel. Of course, I was familiar with hits such as 'Voy a empezar de nuevo' and 'Volverán'. I met her forty-six years after her triumph, and she still looked stunning, glamorous, a star.

Then there's Patricia Kaas, a French performer I admire not just for her voice, but also for her energy. There aren't many female singers who subject themselves time and again to the stresses of a world tour. She was even the first Western female singer to perform in Hanoi after the Vietnam War. When I visited her backstage in Vienna, she was already in her dressing gown. Obviously, I'd never have asked her for a photo, but she simply turned the situation on its head and took her own selfie of the two of us. Patricia told me how, in 2005, she'd sung her winning song 'Herz eines Kämpfers' in the German heat for the Eurovision Song Contest in front of an audience of millions. 'I spent many years working in Saarbrücken when I was young. Singing in German is easy for me.' The same goes for Russian, English and, of course, French. It was in that language that she competed in the 2009 Eurovision Song Contest in Moscow. What nicer way to spend my time than in swapping experiences with such incredible female singers, I thought to myself after our meeting.

Singing is what gives me my greatest pleasure, and when I'm on stage at music events such as the Malta Song Festival or Albania's Festival i Këngës, I feel in harmony with my inner self. Another thing I'll keep up is my love of haute couture, perhaps because my grandmother always attached such great importance to a neat appearance. 'It's a mark of respect to others,' she used to tell me. And also because fashion is art on people. When I sing 'we can be so beautiful', I mean two things: we can be beautiful from within, like when we shine because we've decided on the right path, because we've rejected hate and turned to love. Yet we can enhance our inner beauty from without. This is where fashion comes in. That's its job. That's why I'm passionate about it. And it's with this same commitment that I'm going to turn my attention to a third role: politics. I'll continue to get involved in the effort to highlight injustices and to motivate people to do something about them. It looks like I've got my work cut out for me.

EPILOGUE

The night before the grand final of the Eurovision Song Contest, I stood in front of the mirror in my hotel room. My face half free of makeup, I asked myself: 'Who am I?' I thought about how I'd be going on stage the following evening, and racked my brain trying to think what I might say in the unlikely event that I won. The question 'Who am I?' also tied in to another question that had occupied me since my early childhood: 'Why am *I* the one seeing through these eyes?' 'Who am I?' is *the* philosophical conundrum that has occupied people for thousands of years, and I believe the question about seeing through these eyes can lead us to the answer: when I look at the world through my eyes and with my emotional reactions, that's what creates my personhood. I want to share four snapshots that have helped piece together the puzzle of who I am.

I'm eight-years-old, and am looking out through the net

curtains in my bedroom onto the garage driveway. Although the first snow has fallen, there are still leaves showing through everywhere. *Freeze.* I capture the scene and store it away in my brain, where it becomes *picture number one*.

Bad Mitterndorf is a musical town where people know how to party. I'm twelve years old, and, like every Wednesday, there's a concert taking place in the park. My parents are in charge of the catering, and my father has set up a stall to look like a pretty little house. I stand there, gazing into the empty space. And, all of a sudden, I know: this is *picture number two*.

We're driving through a forest, 'we' being my grandmother, who's behind the wheel, my brother, my two cousins and me. Sitting at the window, I spot the deer. I'm the only one who can see it, and I don't tell any of the others about it – because I know: this is *picture number three*.

The night before the Eurovision Song Contest final, I had these three pictures going through my head like a slideshow: click, picture number one. Click, picture number two. Click, picture number three. And, suddenly, I knew: the day I find picture number four, I'll have the answer to why it's *me* seeing through these eyes. On that day, I'll have the final piece of the puzzle, and I'll know who I am.

I really wasn't expecting to come across picture number four any time soon. The first three pictures are memories from childhood. As far as I was concerned, it might well be late in my life before the missing fourth picture put in an appearance. Even so, absolutely everything had been possible in recent months. I'd experienced more than I could ever have imagined, even in my wildest dreams. And so the inevitable happened. I'd just come from an engagement in

Vienna. I don't remember what it was. As ever, I felt both elated and tired, so I was glad the taxi driver had no problem with my address. There was no 'Where's that then?' or 'Can you tell me how to get there?' He simply started his meter and drove off, while I sank into the comfy seat in the back. Soon after, the taxi turned into Ringstrasse, drove along the Stadtpark, and then into Schubertring, a route I'd taken countless times before. At Schwarzenbergplatz, we saw the Hotel Imperial ahead, a magnificent building from the distant past, a former palace of Duke Philipp of Württemberg. My gaze wandered up the facade to the roof, where, fluttering in the breeze, was the red-white-red flag of Austria.

'Why is it fluttering in slow motion?' I murmured, but the driver didn't answer, probably because he didn't know what I was talking about. In that moment I knew: *this is picture number four*. The Austrian flag. I was surprised at first, I'll admit. A garage driveway in winter, the empty space in a park, a deer at the edge of a forest – these are images resonating with symbolism for me, yet probably not for most other people. But the Austrian flag, that's something else. Picture number four is clearly in a different league. Suddenly I was wide-awake, all my tiredness seemed to have vanished. I could sense a feeling of immense joy spreading through my entire body. The flag, the symbol of my country – of course. It's a place I can call my own: it's where I was born, where I'm at home, where I live, for better or for worse. I sang for Austria at the Eurovision Song Contest, and I'll continue to stand up for Austria in the future. I love Europe and its diverse cultures, I'm a citizen of the world through and through, with a place in my heart for all of humanity.

Yet Austria is and will remain my homeland – and I'm proud of it.